What the Facts Are You Talking About?

All rights are reserved 2024 by Life Style Daily. No part of this publication may be reproduced, stored in a retrieval system or transmitted in any form or by any means, electronic, mechanical, photocopying, recording or otherwise, without prior permission.

Table of Contents

Chapter 1: Mysteries of the Universe 6

- Subchapter 1.1: Galaxies and Black Holes 6
- Subchapter 1.2: Planets and Moons of the Solar System 7
- Subchapter 1.3: Stars and Supernovae 8
- Subchapter 1.4: Time and Space 10
- Subchapter 1.5: Theories on the Origin of the Universe 11

Chapter 2: Extraordinary Facts About Nature 14

- Subchapter 2.1: Weather Phenomena 14
- Subchapter 2.2: Extraordinary Life Forms on Earth 15
- Subchapter 2.3: Rare and Unique Ecosystems 16
- Subchapter 2.4: Discoveries on the Ocean Floor 18
- Subchapter 2.5: Mysteries of Plants and Their Adaptations 20

Chapter 3: The Human Mind and Body 22

- Subchapter 3.1: The Brain and Its Abilities 22
- Subchapter 3.2: Humans and Their Senses 23
- Subchapter 3.3: The Strangest Disorders and Mutations 25
- Subchapter 3.4: Human Body Records 26
- Subchapter 3.5: Human Evolution 28

Chapter 4: The Astonishing History of the World 30

- Subchapter 4.1: The Earliest Civilizations and Their Discoveries 30
- Subchapter 4.2: Cultures and Their Lost Cities 31
- Subchapter 4.3: Famous Battles and Their Mysteries 33
- Subchapter 4.4: Famous Rulers and Their Secrets 35
- Subchapter 4.5: Intriguing Inventions and Discoveries 37

Chapter 5: Amazing Animals 39

- Subchapter 5.1: Predators and Their Hunting Strategies 39
- Subchapter 5.2: The Oldest and Smallest Species 40
- Subchapter 5.3: Animal Records and Oddities 42
- Subchapter 5.4: Animals and Their Intelligence 43
- Subchapter 5.5: Unusual Symbioses and Adaptations 45

Chapter 6: People Who Changed the World 47

- Subchapter 6.1: Inventors and Their Breakthroughs 47
- Subchapter 6.2: The Greatest Scientific Minds 48
- Subchapter 6.3: Visionary Artists and Their Works 50
- Subchapter 6.4: Pioneers of Exploration and Discovery 52
- Subchapter 6.5: Revolutionaries and Their Ideas 53

Chapter 7: Culture and Civilization 56

- Subchapter 7.1: Extraordinary Traditions and Rituals 56
- Subchapter 7.2: The Strangest Religions and Beliefs 57
- Subchapter 7.3: World Cuisines and Their Specialties 59
- Subchapter 7.4: Dances, Art, and Music of Different Cultures 61
- Subchapter 7.5: Famous Buildings and Their History 62

Chapter 8: Mysteries of Science 65

- Subchapter 8.1: Experiments That Changed the World 65
- Subchapter 8.2: The Most Controversial Scientific Theories 66
- Subchapter 8.3: Genetics and Unusual Mutations 68
- Subchapter 8.4: Breakthroughs in Medicine and Their Effects 70
- Subchapter 8.5: Incredible Laws of Physics 72

Chapter 9: Technologies of the Future 74

•Subchapter 9.1: Artificial Intelligence and Robotics 74

•Subchapter 9.2: The Future of Space Travel 75

•Subchapter 9.3: Nanotechnology and Its Applications 77

•Subchapter 9.4: Renewable Energy and Eco-Innovations............. 79

•Subchapter 9.5: Military Technologies and Their Development 80

Chapter 10: Daily Life and Surprising Facts 83

•Subchapter 10.1: The Strangest Guinness World Records 83

•Subchapter 10.2: Origins of Popular Phrases and Sayings 84

•Subchapter 10.3: Everyday Items and Their Unknown Histories ... 86

•Subchapter 10.4: Unusual Laws and Regulations Around the World 88

•Subsection 10.5: Fascinating Facts About Human Customs 89

Chapter 5: Amazing Animals 39
- Subchapter 5.1: Predators and Their Hunting Strategies 39
- Subchapter 5.2: The Oldest and Smallest Species 40
- Subchapter 5.3: Animal Records and Oddities 42
- Subchapter 5.4: Animals and Their Intelligence 43
- Subchapter 5.5: Unusual Symbioses and Adaptations 45

Chapter 6: People Who Changed the World 47
- Subchapter 6.1: Inventors and Their Breakthroughs 47
- Subchapter 6.2: The Greatest Scientific Minds 48
- Subchapter 6.3: Visionary Artists and Their Works 50
- Subchapter 6.4: Pioneers of Exploration and Discovery 52
- Subchapter 6.5: Revolutionaries and Their Ideas 53

Chapter 7: Culture and Civilization 56
- Subchapter 7.1: Extraordinary Traditions and Rituals 56
- Subchapter 7.2: The Strangest Religions and Beliefs 57
- Subchapter 7.3: World Cuisines and Their Specialties 59
- Subchapter 7.4: Dances, Art, and Music of Different Cultures 61
- Subchapter 7.5: Famous Buildings and Their History 62

Chapter 8: Mysteries of Science 65
- Subchapter 8.1: Experiments That Changed the World 65
- Subchapter 8.2: The Most Controversial Scientific Theories 66
- Subchapter 8.3: Genetics and Unusual Mutations 68
- Subchapter 8.4: Breakthroughs in Medicine and Their Effects 70
- Subchapter 8.5: Incredible Laws of Physics 72

Chapter 9: Technologies of the Future 74

    •Subchapter 9.1: Artificial Intelligence and Robotics 74

    •Subchapter 9.2: The Future of Space Travel 75

    •Subchapter 9.3: Nanotechnology and Its Applications 77

    •Subchapter 9.4: Renewable Energy and Eco-Innovations............. 79

    •Subchapter 9.5: Military Technologies and Their Development 80

Chapter 10: Daily Life and Surprising Facts 83

    •Subchapter 10.1: The Strangest Guinness World Records 83

    •Subchapter 10.2: Origins of Popular Phrases and Sayings 84

    •Subchapter 10.3: Everyday Items and Their Unknown Histories ... 86

    •Subchapter 10.4: Unusual Laws and Regulations Around the World 88

    •Subsection 10.5: Fascinating Facts About Human Customs 89

All rights are reserved 2024 by Life Style Daily. No part of this publication may be reproduced, stored in a retrieval system or transmitted in any form or by any means, electronic, mechanical, photocopying, recording or otherwise, without prior permission.

Chapter 1: Mysteries of the Universe

•Subchapter 1.1: Galaxies and Black Holes

Our Galaxy – The Milky Way: The Milky Way is about 100,000 light-years in diameter and contains between 100 and 400 billion stars.

The Oldest Galaxy: GN-z11 is the oldest known galaxy, located around 13.4 billion light-years from Earth—almost as old as the universe itself.

Black Holes: Black holes are objects with such immense mass that their gravitational force prevents even light from escaping.

The Supermassive Black Hole at the Center of the Milky Way: Called Sagittarius A*, it has a mass over 4 million times that of our Sun.

Spiral and Elliptical Galaxies: Spiral galaxies, like the Milky Way, have distinctly outlined arms. Elliptical galaxies are more dispersed and often older.

Galaxy Collisions: Galaxies can collide and merge—a process that takes millions of years. In about 4 billion years, the Milky Way will merge with the Andromeda galaxy.

Light Bending Around Black Holes: A phenomenon known as "gravitational lensing" causes black holes to bend light passing nearby.

Hypervelocity Ejected Stars: Black holes can eject stars at speeds up to 10 million kilometers per hour in a process known as gravitational slingshot.

The Famous Black Hole M87: The first-ever photograph of a black hole's shadow was taken in 2019, of M87, which is 53 million light-years away from us.

Dwarf Galaxies: Small galaxies containing only a few billion stars orbit larger galaxies like the Milky Way.

Pervasive Dark Matter: In every galaxy, 85% of the mass is invisible dark matter, which influences the motion and behavior of galaxies.

Radio Galaxies: Some galaxies emit massive amounts of radio waves due to the presence of active black holes.

The Andromeda Galaxy: As the nearest large galaxy to the Milky Way, it's approaching us at a speed of 110 kilometers per second.

Stars Ejected by Black Holes: Occasionally, black holes eject stars from the galaxy, creating so-called "runaway stars."

Age of Galaxies: Most galaxies in the observable universe are between 1 and 10 billion years old.

Galaxy Formation: Galaxies began forming around 400 million years after the Big Bang.

Galactic Magnetic Fields: Galaxies have magnetic fields that interact with particles moving within them.

Active Galaxies: In some galaxies, the central black hole consumes material, releasing intense energy, classifying them as active galaxies.

"Empty" Galaxies: Some galaxies are nearly empty, with very few stars and dark matter, and are referred to as "ultra-diffuse."

Quasars: Quasars are the brightest objects in the universe, formed by supermassive black holes consuming gas.

•Subchapter 1.2: Planets and Moons of the Solar System

Mercury – Closest to the Sun: Mercury is the smallest planet in the Solar System and the closest to the Sun. It experiences extreme temperature variations, from -173°C at night to 427°C during the day.

A Day on Venus: A day on Venus is longer than its year—Venus rotates so slowly that one rotation takes 243 Earth days.

Earth's Moon: The Moon is Earth's only natural satellite and is moving away from us by about 3.8 cm per year.

Mars and Its Red Color: Mars gets its red color from the high concentration of iron oxide (rust) on its surface.

Olympus Mons on Mars: Mars is home to the tallest mountain in the Solar System—Olympus Mons, a volcano that stands around 22 km high.

The Asteroid Belt: Between Mars and Jupiter lies the asteroid belt, filled with a variety of rocky and metallic objects.

Jupiter – The Gas Giant: Jupiter is the largest planet in the Solar System, with over 75 moons, including the largest one, Ganymede.

The Great Red Spot: Jupiter has a massive storm, the Great Red Spot, which is larger than Earth and has lasted at least 400 years.

Europa – Jupiter's Icy Moon: Europa, one of Jupiter's moons, has an icy crust beneath which there may be an ocean of liquid water.

Saturn and Its Rings: Saturn has the most spectacular rings, made mostly of ice and rock, extending thousands of kilometers.

Titan – Saturn's Moon: Titan, Saturn's largest moon, has a dense atmosphere and rivers of liquid methane and ethane.

Uranus – The Tilted Planet: Uranus is unique for its tilted rotation axis, lying nearly in the plane of its orbit, giving it the appearance of "lying on its side."

Unusual Seasons on Uranus: Each season on Uranus lasts about 21 Earth years.

Neptune and Its Intense Winds: Neptune has the strongest winds in the Solar System, reaching speeds of up to 1,300 miles per hour (2,100 km/h).

Triton – Neptune's Moon: Triton, Neptune's largest moon, orbits in the opposite direction of the planet's rotation, a unique trait in the Solar System.

Dwarf Planet Pluto: Although reclassified as a dwarf planet, Pluto has its own moons, the largest of which is Charon.

Ice Giants – Uranus and Neptune: Unlike Jupiter and Saturn, Uranus and Neptune contain large amounts of water ice, ammonia, and methane.

Martian Moons – Phobos and Deimos: Mars has two small moons, Phobos and Deimos, which are irregularly shaped and resemble asteroids.

Eris – The Distant World: Eris is a dwarf planet beyond Pluto, nearly the same size and one of the largest bodies in the Kuiper Belt.

The Kuiper Belt: The Kuiper Belt is a region beyond Neptune's orbit filled with icy objects, from which some comets originate.

•Subchapter 1.3: Stars and Supernovae

Star Formation: Stars are born in clouds of gas and dust called nebulae, where gravity causes the material to collapse and form a protostar.

Lifespan of Stars: Stars live for billions of years—the more massive the star, the shorter its lifespan.

Our Sun as a Yellow Dwarf Star: The Sun is a yellow dwarf, an average-sized star with a surface temperature of about 5,500°C (9,932°F).

Red Giants: When a star exhausts its fuel, it expands into a red giant. This will happen to the Sun in about 5 billion years.

White Dwarfs: After shedding its outer layers, a red giant leaves behind a hot core called a white dwarf, which gradually cools over time.

Neutron Stars: When a massive star collapses, it can form an incredibly dense neutron star—just a teaspoon of its material would weigh billions of tons.

Pulsars: Pulsars are rapidly spinning neutron stars that emit beams of radiation, appearing to "pulse" like a lighthouse.

Supernovae: When a massive star reaches the end of its life, it explodes as a supernova, releasing immense energy and scattering elements into space.

Types of Supernovae: Supernovae are classified as Type I (when a star accumulates matter from a companion) and Type II (resulting from the collapse of a massive star).

Crab Nebula: This is the remnant of a supernova observed in 1054, containing a pulsar that emits strong radiation.

Hypernovae: Even more powerful than supernovae, hypernovae occur from the collapse of especially massive stars.

Binary Stars: Most stars exist in binary or multiple star systems, where they orbit each other due to gravitational pull.

Brown Dwarfs: Brown dwarfs are "failed" stars—they did not accumulate enough mass to start nuclear fusion and shine like other stars.

Star Death and Heavy Elements: Heavy elements like gold are created in supernova explosions and spread throughout space.

The Largest Known Star – UY Scuti: UY Scuti is one of the largest known stars, with a diameter over 1,700 times that of the Sun.

Slow and Fast Rotating Stars: A star's rotation speed affects its shape—fast-rotating stars become more flattened.

Blue Giants: These stars are massive and hot, shine with a blue light, and have short, intense lifespans.

Iron – The End of Fusion for Stars: When a star forms iron in its core, it can no longer sustain fusion, leading to a collapse and often a supernova explosion.

Cepheids – Variable Stars: Cepheids are variable stars with regularly pulsing brightness, allowing astronomers to measure cosmic distances accurately.

Kilonovae: A rare event where two neutron stars collide, creating a powerful explosion and producing elements like gold and platinum.

•Subchapter 1.4: Time and Space

Einstein's Theory of Relativity: Albert Einstein explained that time and space are interconnected and can be warped by the presence of mass and energy.

Gravity and Time: The stronger the gravity, the slower time flows—a phenomenon known as time dilation, observed near massive objects like black holes.

Speed of Light: Light travels at approximately 300,000 km/s (186,000 miles per second) in a vacuum, the maximum speed possible in the universe.

Time Dilation at High Speeds: According to relativity, the faster one moves, the slower time passes relative to observers at rest.

The Big Bang – Beginning of Time and Space: The universe began with the Big Bang about 13.8 billion years ago, marking the origin of time, space, matter, and energy.

Einstein's Equation: The famous equation $E=mc^2$ expresses the relationship between mass (m) and energy (E), where "c" is the speed of light, showing that mass and energy are interchangeable.

Spacetime: Spacetime is a four-dimensional structure where three dimensions of space and one of time are combined into a unified "fabric" of the universe.

Tachyons – Hypothetical Particles: Tachyons are theoretical particles that would travel faster than light, though their existence remains unproven.

Black Holes and Time Dilation: Near black holes, time slows dramatically compared to regions with weaker gravity—this has inspired many theories about time travel.

Wormholes: A wormhole is a hypothetical shortcut between two points in spacetime, potentially allowing travel across vast distances.

Cosmic Time: In cosmic terms, light-years are used as a unit of distance—the distance light travels in one year, approximately 9.46 trillion kilometers (5.88 trillion miles).

Cosmic Inflation: Shortly after the Big Bang, the universe underwent a rapid expansion phase, where its size multiplied many times in a fraction of a second.

The Universe Keeps Expanding: Edwin Hubble discovered that galaxies are moving apart, indicating the universe is expanding.

No Center of Space: The universe is expanding everywhere simultaneously, meaning there is no central point of expansion.

Twin Paradox: In relativity, a twin traveling at high speed ages more slowly than a twin who remains on Earth.

No Absolute Time: Einstein's relativity asserts there is no single universal time that flows the same for all observers.

Cosmic Microwave Background (CMB): This radiation is the "afterglow" of the Big Bang, visible as a uniform microwave background throughout the universe.

Does the Universe Have a Shape?: Scientists speculate on the shape of the universe; it could be flat, spherical, or another form, depending on its density.

Cosmic Horizon: The horizon marks the farthest distance we can observe in the universe, limited by the time it takes light to reach us.

The "Arrow of Time": The direction of time's flow—from past to future—is called the "arrow of time" and aligns with the second law of thermodynamics.

•Subchapter 1.5: Theories on the Origin of the Universe

The Big Bang Theory: The most widely accepted theory suggests the universe began about 13.8 billion years ago from a point of infinite density and temperature, which suddenly began to expand.

Cosmic Inflation: According to this theory, fractions of a second after the Big Bang, the universe underwent a rapid expansion, growing exponentially in an extremely short time.

Steady State Theory: Popular in the 1940s, this theory proposed that the universe has always existed without a beginning or end. Matter continually forms to fill the void as the universe expands.

Oscillating Universe Theory: This theory posits that the universe goes through cycles of expansion and contraction—after each Big Bang, there follows a Big Crunch, then another Big Bang.

Big Bounce Theory: According to this concept, the universe emerged from a previous cycle, collapsing to a point of maximum density before "bouncing" into a new phase of expansion.

Brane Cosmology: In string theory, our universe is a membrane (brane) in a higher-dimensional space. A collision between branes could have sparked the birth of our universe.

The Multiverse Theory: This theory suggests the existence of multiple universes, each with its own laws of physics; our universe is one of many that may continuously arise and fade.

Bubble Universe Theory: In this model, our universe is a "bubble" within a vast multiverse, where each bubble forms through quantum tunneling in a vacuum.

Plasma Model: This theory proposes that the universe was created through plasma dynamics, where electromagnetic forces play a crucial role in shaping the universe instead of gravity.

Ekpyrotic Theory: This theory suggests that our universe was formed from a collision between two higher-dimensional branes in space.

Quantum Vacuum Theory: This theory proposes that the universe emerged from quantum fluctuations in a vacuum, where random energy spikes gave rise to our universe.

Loop Quantum Gravity: This theory suggests spacetime has a discrete structure with no beginning; time may have always existed, with the universe undergoing continual cycles.

Holographic Theory: This theory posits that our universe could be a hologram—a projection of events from a lower-dimensional space.

Universe as a Simulation: This theory speculates that the universe might be an advanced simulation created by a higher intelligence, similar to a computer simulation.

Cosmic Chaos Theory: This concept proposes that the universe emerged as a random result of a chaotic state, from which physical laws took shape.

The Anti-Universe Theory: According to this theory, a mirror universe made of antimatter was created parallel to ours at the beginning of time.

Quantum Universe: This theory suggests the universe is a product of quantum processes, where quantum states appear and disappear within space.

Baum-Frampton Model: This theory proposes an endless cycle of cosmic expansion and contraction, where matter transforms in each cycle, avoiding complete loss of information.

Fractal Universe: Some scientists believe the universe may have a fractal structure, with infinite, self-similar structures at different scales.

Higher-Dimensional Universe (String Theory): String theory proposes that the universe consists of 11 dimensions, and what we observe is only one aspect of this complex structure.

Chapter 2: Extraordinary Facts About Nature

•Subchapter 2.1: Weather Phenomena

Volcanic Lightning: During volcanic eruptions, lightning forms due to the accumulation of electric charges in the ash and gases ejected by the volcano.

Ball Lightning: This rare and mysterious phenomenon involves a glowing ball of light, ranging from a few centimeters to several inches in diameter, often appearing during thunderstorms.

Ice Tsunamis: In cold regions, sudden temperature increases and strong winds can push large amounts of frozen water in an "ice tsunami," destroying everything in its path.

Fire Tornadoes: During wildfires, fire can swirl into tornado-like structures, reaching temperatures above 1,000°C (1,832°F).

White Rainbows (Fog Bows): Similar to regular rainbows, but occurring in foggy conditions. Due to smaller water droplets, fog bows appear with a faint, pale color.

Catatumbo Lightning: Over Lake Maracaibo in Venezuela, lightning strikes most of the year, often without accompanying rain—a unique and intense display.

Fish Rain: In places like Honduras, small fish sometimes fall from the sky during intense storms, likely lifted by strong winds.

Supercell Thunderstorms: These are massive, long-lasting storms that can persist for hours and often spawn destructive tornadoes and tennis-ball-sized hail.

Aurora Borealis and Aurora Australis: The northern and southern lights, seen in polar regions, occur when solar wind particles interact with Earth's atmosphere.

Light Pillars: Created when light reflects off ice crystals suspended in the atmosphere, producing vertical columns of light in the air.

Sea Fog and Warm Seas: When warm air passes over a cooler sea surface, it creates dense fog, commonly seen in coastal areas.

Giant Hailstorms: In some regions, hailstorms produce ice balls weighing over a kilogram (2.2 pounds).

Blood Rain: This occurs when winds carry dust or sand particles from deserts into the atmosphere, coloring the rain with a reddish tint.

Virga – Vanishing Rain: Rain that evaporates before reaching the ground, creating the visual effect of "disappearing" rain in the sky.

Red Fog: Forms when dust or sand particles mix with moisture in the air, giving the fog a reddish hue.

Ice Flowers: Delicate ice formations resembling flowers can develop on the sea surface in extremely cold temperatures.

Sand and Dust Storms: Dust storms can travel thousands of kilometers, with Saharan dust reaching as far as the Amazon, where it enriches the soil with nutrients.

Waterspouts: These are rotating columns of water over the ocean, resembling tornadoes, and can lift water and small organisms into the air.

Haboobs – Desert Dust Storms: Haboobs are intense sandstorms typical of desert areas like the Sahara and Arabian Desert.

Sun Halos: Sun halos form when sunlight passes through ice crystals in the upper atmosphere, creating rings around the sun.

•Subchapter 2.2: Extraordinary Life Forms on Earth

Tardigrades (Water Bears): These microscopic creatures can survive extreme conditions—from freezing temperatures to 150°C heat, radiation, and even the vacuum of space.

Axolotl: This unusual amphibian never fully undergoes metamorphosis, retaining larval traits for life, and can regenerate its limbs.

Deep-Sea Shrimp from Hydrothermal Vents: Living on the ocean floor near geothermal vents, these shrimp endure extremely high temperatures.

Master Camouflagers – Cephalopods: Octopuses, squids, and cuttlefish can change their skin color and texture to blend in or scare off predators.

Pangolin: The only mammal covered in scales, pangolins use their long tongues to hunt ants and termites.

Microbes in Movile Cave: In a Romanian cave isolated from light and oxygen for millions of years, bacteria survive on chemical processes instead of photosynthesis.

The Blob – Physarum polycephalum: This single-celled organism can move, "learn," and make decisions despite lacking a brain.

Wood Frog (Rana sylvatica): This frog can survive being frozen in winter, halting its biological processes until it thaws.

Tarsiers: These small primates have large eyes adapted for night vision and are the only entirely carnivorous primates.

Blobfish (Psychrolutes marcidus): Living at great depths, this fish has a gelatinous body that helps it withstand high pressures.

Immortal Jellyfish (Turritopsis dohrnii): Known as "immortal," this jellyfish can revert to its juvenile state and effectively regenerate.

Vampire Squid (Vampyroteuthis infernalis): This unusual creature lives in the deep ocean and is adapted to low-oxygen environments.

Glass Frog: With translucent skin, this frog's internal organs, including its beating heart, are visible.

Mudskipper: This fish can move on land using its fins and breathe through its skin, allowing it to spend much of its time above water.

Blue Whale: The largest animal ever to exist, a blue whale can reach up to 30 meters (98 feet) in length and weigh up to 180 tons.

Toxin-Resistant Ants: In the Amazon rainforest, a species of ants survives in nests among leaves that are toxic to most other creatures.

Amazonian Velvet Worms (Onychophora): These worms shoot a sticky substance to immobilize their prey, making hunting easier.

Reef Sponges: Some reef sponges can live for thousands of years, making them among the oldest known organisms on Earth.

Survivalist Cockroaches: Cockroaches are highly resilient and can survive extreme conditions, including radiation and high doses of toxins.

Anableps (Four-Eyed Fish): This fish has eyes divided into two parts, enabling it to see both above and below the water simultaneously.

•Subchapter 2.3: Rare and Unique Ecosystems

Deep-Sea Hydrothermal Vents: Found on the ocean floor, these vents release mineral-rich hot water from Earth's interior, creating a unique ecosystem of organisms adapted to extreme, sunless conditions.

Mangrove Root Rainforests: Mangroves grow along tropical coastlines, with roots extending above the water, creating a vital habitat for fish, crustaceans, and birds.

Namib Desert: One of the oldest deserts in the world, home to organisms adapted to extreme conditions, including beetles that collect moisture from fog and drought-resistant plants.

Galapagos Biosphere: This isolated archipelago, with its high level of endemism, is home to unique species like giant tortoises, marine iguanas, and Darwin's finches that evolved in distinctive ways.

Amazon – Earth's Green Lungs: The world's largest rainforest, it houses thousands of plant and animal species and plays a crucial role in regulating the global climate.

Kelp Forests: Underwater "forests" in cold ocean waters, created by kelp, which provides shelter and food for fish, crustaceans, and seabirds.

Movile Cave in Romania: Sealed off from the surface for millions of years, this cave hosts unique microorganisms that survive in total darkness without fresh air.

Salar de Uyuni Salt Flats: The world's largest salt flat in Bolivia turns into a massive mirror during the rainy season, with saline waters rich in lithium.

Great Barrier Reef Coral System: The largest coral reef system in the world, home to thousands of species of fish, corals, and other marine life, but threatened by climate change.

Madagascar's Tsingy Granite Formations: Sharp rock formations create natural labyrinths in Madagascar's forests and serve as habitat for endemic species like lemurs and unique birds.

Antarctic Ice Lakes: Beneath Antarctica's ice are lakes isolated for millions of years, containing unique microorganisms surviving in complete darkness.

Lake Natron in Tanzania: With high salinity, pH levels, and temperatures reaching 60°C (140°F), this lake supports life like flamingos that have adapted to these conditions.

Everglades Wetlands: A vast wetland system in Florida, home to alligators, birds, and unique plant species, playing a vital role in the region's ecosystem.

Alkaline Mono Lake in California: This highly alkaline lake supports unique life forms, including algae and brine shrimp, essential to migrating birds.

Siberian Northern Taiga: One of Earth's largest forested areas, full of conifers and home to animals adapted to harsh climates, such as bears and reindeer.

Seamounts: These underwater mountains support diverse marine life, including fish, corals, and plants, forming unique ecosystems in the middle of the ocean.

Baltic Anoxic Zone: The depths of the Baltic Sea contain layers of oxygen-depleted water, where specific anaerobic bacteria thrive.

Florida Mangrove Forests: These forests protect against storms and coastal erosion and host diverse species of fish, crustaceans, and birds.

African Great Lakes: Lakes such as Tanganyika and Victoria are habitats for many endemic fish species found nowhere else on Earth.

Taklamakan Desert Sand Dunes: Located in western China, these desert dunes support life forms uniquely adapted to extremely hot and dry conditions.

•Subchapter 2.4: Discoveries on the Ocean Floor

RMS Titanic Wreck: The wreck of the famous RMS Titanic was discovered in 1985 at a depth of approximately 3,800 meters on the floor of the North Atlantic.

Deep-Sea Hydrothermal Vents: Discovered in the 1970s, these geothermal sources emit mineral-rich hot water and support unique ecosystems that thrive without sunlight.

Abandoned "City" – Yonaguni Monument: Off the coast of Japan, stone formations resembling pyramids have been found, which some scientists speculate may be remnants of an ancient civilization.

Mariana Trench – The Deepest Place on Earth: Located in the western Pacific, the Mariana Trench reaches depths over 11,000 meters and is home to extraordinary organisms.

Deep-Sea Jellyfish and Squid: Research expeditions have uncovered numerous new deep-sea species, including giant squids and bioluminescent jellyfish.

Living Fossils – Coelacanths: Once thought extinct for millions of years, coelacanths were found alive in 1938 off the coasts of Africa and Indonesia.

Sunken Continent Zealandia: Recognized as a "sunken continent" in 2017, Zealandia covers 4.9 million square kilometers beneath the Pacific Ocean.

Ancient Fossils: Fossils of ancient organisms found on the ocean floor provide insights into early geological periods and climates.

Bahama Pyramids: Underwater structures resembling pyramids have been found near the Bahamas, sparking speculation about ancient civilizations.

Chemical Precursors to Life: Traces of chemical compounds, such as amino acids, have been found on the ocean floor, potentially offering clues about the origins of life.

Shipwrecks and Treasures: Numerous shipwrecks, both military and merchant, have been discovered with valuable cargo, including gold, jewelry, and weapons.

Manganese Nodule Fields: Vast fields of manganese nodules on the Pacific Ocean floor may become valuable sources of raw materials.

New Fish and Crab Species: Many new species of fish and crustaceans, including "zombie fish" that live in lightless depths, have been discovered.

Methane Hydrate Fields: Fields of methane hydrate have been located on the ocean floor—a potential energy source with significant climate implications.

Underwater "Waterfalls": Submarine canyons and waterfalls, like the famous one off Greenland's coast, where cold, dense water plunges into the depths, creating massive currents.

Deep-Sea Bacteria and Microorganisms: Bacteria and microorganisms living in extreme conditions have been discovered, aiding research in astrobiology.

Underwater Mountains and Volcanoes: Thousands of underwater mountains and volcanoes provide unique habitats for deep-sea organisms.

Deep-Sea Whale Skeletons: Whale skeletons on the ocean floor attract unique species of worms and other organisms that help decompose these remains.

Submarine Rivers and Lakes: Submarine rivers and lakes filled with hydrogen sulfide-rich water create distinct ecosystems on the ocean floor.

Ice Crystals – "Ice Flowers": At very low temperatures on the ocean floor, ice crystal structures resembling flowers form, supporting unique bacterial life.

Subchapter 2.5: Mysteries of Plants and Their Adaptations

Sundew – Carnivorous Plant: Sundews are carnivorous plants that have evolved to capture and digest insects, allowing them to gain nutrients in nutrient-poor soils.

Baobab – The Bottle Tree: Baobabs can store up to 120,000 liters of water in their trunks, enabling them to survive prolonged droughts.

Welwitschia Mirabilis: This plant from the Namib Desert has just two leaves that grow continuously throughout its life, which can span up to 2,000 years.

The Sensitive Mimosa (Mimosa pudica): Known as the "shy plant," it closes its leaves in response to touch or movement, potentially deterring predators.

Bamboo's Rapid Growth: Certain bamboo species can grow up to 91 cm (3 feet) per day, making them some of the fastest-growing plants on Earth.

Cacti – Water Storage Experts: Cacti have specialized tissues for water storage, and their spines reduce evaporation, helping them endure desert conditions.

Breadvine Climber: This climbing plant uses its long vines to reach sunlight in dense rainforests by scaling trees.

Victoria Amazonica: The giant leaves of this aquatic plant can reach up to 3 meters (10 feet) in diameter and support the weight of an adult.

Rafflesia – The World's Largest Flower: Rafflesia arnoldii produces the largest flower on Earth, reaching up to 1 meter in diameter, and emits a scent of rotting flesh to attract pollinating flies.

Mangrove Aerial Roots: Mangroves develop aerial roots that protrude above the water surface to absorb oxygen in flooded areas.

Venus Flytrap: This carnivorous plant has leaves that snap shut instantly when an insect touches its trigger hairs, trapping the prey.

Camouflaging Orchids: Some orchids mimic the appearance of female insects to attract males, which inadvertently transfer pollen between flowers.

Eucalyptus and Its Oils: Eucalyptus trees produce essential oils that are toxic to most animals, providing protection from herbivores.

Epiphytic Plants: Epiphytes, like orchids and bromeliads, grow on other plants to access more sunlight without harming their hosts.

Agave's Single Bloom: Agave plants bloom only once in their lifetime, producing towering flower stalks before dying.

Air-Purifying Plants: Sansevieria and pothos are examples of plants that can remove toxins from the air, making them popular indoor plants.

Lithops – Living Stones: These succulents resemble stones, camouflaging them from herbivores in desert environments.

Sea Tree – Kelp: Kelp grows in dense underwater "forests" in deep waters, utilizing sunlight that reaches the seafloor.

Corpse Flower: The titan arum flower emits an odor resembling rotting meat to attract pollinating insects—a unique adaptation.

Desert Rose: This plant has thick stems for water storage and leaves that minimize moisture loss, allowing it to endure prolonged droughts.

Chapter 3: The Human Mind and Body

•Subchapter 3.1: The Brain and Its Abilities

Number of Neurons: The human brain contains about 86 billion neurons, forming networks that enable communication and information processing.

Synapses – Connections Between Neurons: Each neuron can form up to 10,000 synapses, creating trillions of connections across the brain, essential for memory and learning.

Brain Plasticity: The brain can change and adapt in response to experiences—a process known as neuroplasticity.

Using Both Hemispheres: While each hemisphere specializes in certain functions (the left in logic, the right in creativity), the brain operates in an integrated way.

Short-Term and Long-Term Memory: The brain stores different types of memory—short-term for a few seconds and long-term potentially for a lifetime.

Hemispheric Dominance: Most people have a dominant hemisphere (usually the left), influencing preferences in logic and language.

Memory Capacity: The brain can store an estimated 2.5 petabytes of information, roughly equivalent to 3 million hours of video.

Broca's and Wernicke's Areas: These brain areas are responsible for speech and language comprehension, and damage to them can lead to speech difficulties.

Hippocampus – Memory Center: The hippocampus is the brain's structure responsible for encoding memories and spatial orientation.

Face Recognition Ability: The brain has a specialized area for recognizing faces, essential for social interactions and relationships.

Visualization and Creativity: The prefrontal cortex allows us to imagine things that don't exist—this region is key to creativity and planning.

Placebo Effect: The brain can induce physiological responses to "medications" with no active ingredients, demonstrating the power of suggestion.

Dreams and Lucid Dreaming: In the REM phase, the brain is active with dream activity, and some people can control their dreams—a phenomenon known as lucid dreaming.

Perception of Time: The brain perceives time subjectively—it seems to pass faster in exciting situations and slower during boredom.

Language Learning Ability: The brain is naturally attuned to learning languages, and children up to around age 7 can learn them without an accent.

Empathy and Mirror Neurons: Mirror neurons allow us to "feel" what others feel, forming the basis for empathy and social understanding.

Perfect Pitch: Some people's brains can identify sounds and musical notes with incredible precision, a skill especially useful in music.

Visual Processing: The brain processes images in just 13 milliseconds, making it highly efficient at pattern recognition.

Intuition: The brain unconsciously processes information, enabling us to make intuitive decisions—sometimes called "fast thinking."

Self-Healing and the Nocebo Effect: In stress, the brain can negatively impact health, but a positive mindset can also accelerate physical recovery.

•Subchapter 3.2: Humans and Their Senses

Sight – The Dominant Sense: Sight is the most important sense for humans, providing about 80% of the information we receive from our environment.

Color Perception: Human vision distinguishes millions of color shades through three types of cones in the retina that are sensitive to red, green, and blue.

Color Blindness: Some people have a genetic variation in cone cells, leading to color blindness, most commonly red-green color deficiency.

Night Vision: Although humans can't see in complete darkness, rod cells in the retina allow us to see better in low light.

Sense of Smell – Scent Memory: The brain can remember scents for decades, closely tied to emotions and memories, as the olfactory area is near the memory center.

Pheromones and Olfactory Chemistry: Smell affects human attraction, with our noses able to detect chemical signals related to genetic compatibility.

Hearing – Response to Sounds: Human hearing detects sound frequencies from 20 Hz to 20 kHz, although sensitivity to higher frequencies declines with age.

Sound Localization Ability: By analyzing differences in timing and intensity between sounds reaching each ear, we can locate the source of a sound.

Absolute and Relative Pitch: Absolute pitch is the ability to identify notes precisely, while relative pitch allows us to distinguish pitches in relation to others.

Touch – Sense of Skin Receptors: Our skin contains millions of receptors that recognize various stimuli, including pressure, heat, cold, and pain.

Pain as a Protective Mechanism: Pain warns the body of tissue damage, but some people lack pain sensitivity, which can be dangerous.

Tactile Memory: Touch is also linked to memory—studies show that touch evokes emotions and plays a key role in social connections.

Taste – Sensitivity to Substances: Humans recognize five basic tastes: sweet, sour, salty, bitter, and umami. Each taste serves a different role in assessing food.

Shaping of Taste Preferences: Our taste preferences develop from early childhood and can change throughout life.

Sense of Balance (Vestibular System): Located in the inner ear, it allows us to maintain balance and spatial orientation.

Proprioception: This is the brain's ability to perceive the position of body parts, even when we can't see them directly.

Temperature Perception: Our skin has heat and cold receptors that help us assess environmental temperature and avoid dangerous situations.

Extreme Touch Sensitivity in Fingertips: Fingertips have the highest concentration of touch receptors, allowing precise actions.

Sense of Presence – "Sixth Sense": Some scientists suggest we can sense the presence of others or changes in surroundings through subconscious cues.

Synesthesia: In some people, senses overlap, such as seeing sounds or tasting colors, adding new dimensions to sensory perception.

Subchapter 3.3: The Strangest Disorders and Mutations

Progeria – Premature Aging Syndrome: This genetic disorder causes rapid aging in children, who often appear elderly and typically live only into their teens.

Werewolf Syndrome (Hypertrichosis): Individuals with this condition have excessive hair growth on the face and body resembling fur, caused by a genetic mutation.

Alien Hand Syndrome: People with this disorder lose control of one hand, which acts independently, often performing actions without the person's intent.

Fibrodysplasia (Muscles Turning to Bone): This condition causes muscles and soft tissues to transform into bone, leading to loss of mobility.

Cotard's Syndrome (Walking Corpse Syndrome): Individuals with this rare disorder believe they are dead or missing internal organs.

Fish Odor Syndrome (Trimethylaminuria): Those affected emit a fishy odor due to the body's inability to break down trimethylamine.

Stone Man Disease (Osteopetrosis): This disease causes abnormally dense and brittle bones, which are prone to fractures and deformities.

Von Willebrand Syndrome (Bleeding Disorder): A genetic condition that affects blood clotting, causing even minor injuries to result in uncontrolled bleeding.

Proteus Syndrome (Elephant Man Syndrome): This disorder causes uncontrolled growth of skin, bones, and tissues; Joseph Merrick, the "Elephant Man," suffered from it.

Immortal Cancer Cells (HeLa Cells): Henrietta Lacks' cancer cells are still used in research due to their ability to divide indefinitely, making them "immortal."

Hemophilia – The Royal Disease: A genetic bleeding disorder that was prevalent among European royal families due to close familial relations.

Polydactyly – Extra Fingers or Toes: A genetic mutation that results in additional fingers or toes, relatively common but varying in form.

Excessive Melanin – Coral Melanosis: This condition results in extremely dark skin, leading to both aesthetic and health complications.

Congenital Analgesia – Absence of Pain: People with this mutation don't feel pain, which, though it may seem advantageous, is dangerous as they're unaware of injuries.

Ectodermal Dysplasia: This disorder affects the development of hair, skin, teeth, and nails, often resulting in an unusual appearance.

Ehlers-Danlos Syndrome: Individuals with this condition have extremely flexible skin and joints, making them susceptible to injuries and joint dislocations.

Turner Syndrome: Affects only females, who have only one X chromosome, leading to short stature, lack of menstruation, and other health issues.

Porphyria – The Vampire Disease: This condition causes extreme sensitivity to sunlight, leading to pale skin and pigmentation issues.

Polymelia – Extra Limbs: A rare mutation causing the growth of additional limbs, intriguing scientists with its implications for regeneration.

Albinism: A genetic condition in which the body produces no melanin, resulting in completely white skin and hair and a pinkish hue to the eyes.

•Subchapter 3.4: Human Body Records

Tallest Person in History: Robert Wadlow, who stood at 272 cm (8 ft 11 in), is recognized as the tallest person to have ever lived.

Shortest Person in History: Chandra Bahadur Dangi from Nepal measured only 54.6 cm (21.5 in) tall, making him the shortest recorded person in history.

Longest Time Without Sleep: Randy Gardner stayed awake for 264 hours (11 days) in 1965, setting the record for voluntary sleeplessness.

Longest Beard: Ram Singh Chauhan from India holds the record with a beard length of 5.6 meters (18 ft 5 in).

Strongest Man: Hafþór Júlíus Björnsson, known as "The Mountain" from Game of Thrones, set a strength record by deadlifting 501 kg (1,104 lbs).

Longest Fingernails: Lee Redmond from the USA grew her nails to a combined length of 8.65 meters (28 ft 4 in) before they were broken in an accident.

Fastest 100-Meter Sprint: Usain Bolt ran 100 meters in 9.58 seconds, a record he set in 2009 that remains unbeaten.

Heaviest Person: Jon Brower Minnoch reached a weight of 635 kg (1,400 lbs), the highest recorded weight in history.

Deepest Free Dive: Herbert Nitsch reached a depth of 253 meters (830 ft) in the "no limits" freediving category, setting a world record.

Oldest Documented Person: Jeanne Calment from France lived to be 122 years and 164 days, the longest confirmed human lifespan.

Longest Long Jump: Mike Powell set the long jump record at 8.95 meters (29 ft 4.25 in) in 1991.

Most Flexible Person: Daniel Browning Smith, known as "Rubberboy," is considered the most flexible person, able to contort his body into incredible positions.

Most Tattoos: Lucky Diamond Rich from Australia has tattoos covering 100% of his body, including his eyeballs.

Highest Recorded Body Temperature: Willie Jones survived a body temperature of 46.5°C (115.7°F) after suffering from heatstroke.

Longest Breath Held Underwater: Budimir Šobat held his breath underwater for an astonishing 24 minutes and 37 seconds, setting the record.

Most Squats: Minoru Yoshida set a stamina record by completing 10,507 squats without a break.

Fastest Growth in Height: Robert Wadlow, the tallest person in history, grew to 2.5 meters (8 ft 2 in) by age 17.

Highest Cold Endurance: Wim Hof, known as "The Iceman," spent over an hour submerged in ice water, setting a record for cold endurance.

Largest Waist Circumference: Walter Hudson from the USA had a waist circumference of 300 cm (118 in), one of the most extraordinary records.

Most Swords Swallowed: Dan Meyer holds the world record for swallowing 21 swords simultaneously in this unusual feat.

Subchapter 3.5: Human Evolution

Oldest Ancestor – Sahelanthropus Tchadensis: Sahelanthropus, living around 7 million years ago, is one of the oldest known human ancestors, already showing traits of bipedalism.

Australopithecus: Australopithecines, such as Australopithecus afarensis, lived around 4 million years ago, moving bipedally yet still adept at climbing trees.

Homo Habilis – "Handy Man": Homo habilis, who lived around 2.4–1.4 million years ago, is considered the first hominin to use stone tools.

Homo Erectus – The First Migrant: Homo erectus was the first hominin species to leave Africa, spreading into Europe and Asia around 1.9 million years ago.

Neanderthals: Neanderthals inhabited Europe and Asia, coexisting with Homo sapiens. They adapted well to cold climates and displayed advanced skills, such as tool-making and fire use.

Interbreeding with Neanderthals: Modern humans carry 1–2% Neanderthal DNA, indicating interbreeding between Homo sapiens and Neanderthals.

Homo Floresiensis – "The Hobbit": Discovered on the Indonesian island of Flores, Homo floresiensis was notably small, resembling a "hobbit," and lived as recently as 50,000 years ago.

Homo Sapiens – Emergence of Modern Humans: Homo sapiens appeared in Africa around 300,000 years ago, distinguished by advanced tools and communication abilities.

Cognitive Revolution: About 70,000 years ago, humans developed complex thinking, enabling language, beliefs, and culture.

Out of Africa Migration: Around 60–70,000 years ago, Homo sapiens began a major migration out of Africa, populating Europe, Asia, Australia, and the Americas.

First Complex Tools: Homo sapiens excelled in creating complex tools from bone, stone, and wood, which significantly improved hunting and gathering.

Cave Art: Paintings in European and Asian caves, dating back about 40,000 years, demonstrate advanced abstract thinking and artistic expression.

Mastery of Fire: Homo erectus was the first hominin species to master fire, which allowed cooking, protection, and survival in colder climates.

Genetic Diversity: The greatest genetic diversity is found in Africa, confirming it as humanity's birthplace.

Domestication of Animals: Around 15,000 years ago, humans began domesticating animals like dogs, impacting lifestyle and social relations.

Agricultural Development: The Neolithic Revolution around 10,000 years ago enabled agriculture, leading to settlements and the beginnings of civilization.

Formation of Culture: With the development of language and abstract thinking, Homo sapiens began creating cultures, traditions, and religions, setting them apart from earlier species.

Rise of Cities: The first cities, such as Uruk, emerged around 5,000 years ago, initiating an era of civilization and complex social structures.

Technological Progress: Over centuries, Homo sapiens developed increasingly advanced technology—from stone tools to metalworking and eventually the Industrial Revolution.

Cultural Evolution: Modern human evolution is largely cultural and technological, profoundly shaping the lives and environments of Homo sapiens.

Chapter 4: The Astonishing History of the World

- ## Subchapter 4.1: The Earliest Civilizations and Their Discoveries

Sumerians – Invention of Cuneiform Writing: The Sumerians of Mesopotamia created the first known writing system, cuneiform, around 3400 BCE, enabling the development of administration and literature.

Egypt – Construction of the Pyramids: The ancient Egyptians built monumental structures, including the Great Pyramid of Giza, one of the Seven Wonders of the Ancient World that still stands today.

Indus Valley Civilization – Urban Planning: The Indus Valley Civilization (c. 3300–1300 BCE) showcased advanced urban planning and sewage systems in cities like Mohenjo-Daro and Harappa.

China – Bronze Casting: The Shang Dynasty (c. 1600–1046 BCE) was one of the earliest civilizations to use bronze for weaponry and tools, advancing their military technology.

Phoenicians – The Phoenician Alphabet: The Phoenicians invented the first alphabet, which was simple and effective and became the basis for modern alphabets like Greek and Latin.

Mesopotamia – Irrigation Systems: The Sumerians and Babylonians developed sophisticated irrigation systems to control water flow from the Tigris and Euphrates rivers, enabling large-scale agriculture.

Minoans – Palace of Knossos: On Crete, the Minoan civilization built the Palace of Knossos, featuring advanced sewage systems and serving as an administrative and cultural center.

Maya – The Mayan Calendar: The Maya developed a precise calendar that accounted for astronomical cycles, predicting celestial events with great accuracy.

Akkad – The First Empire: Sargon the Great of Akkad created the world's first known empire around 2334 BCE, uniting various city-states of Mesopotamia under one rule.

Hittites – Ironworking: The Hittites were among the first to master ironworking, which gave them a military advantage and advanced their civilization's technology.

Persia – Royal Roads: The Persians built an extensive road network connecting their empire, enabling fast communication and long-distance trade.

Olmecs – Monumental Sculptures: The Olmecs, regarded as Mesoamerica's first civilization, created colossal stone heads, likely representing their rulers.

Ancient Greece – Athenian Democracy: Athens established the first known form of democracy, where citizens could vote on political and public issues.

Etruscans – Sewage Systems: The Etruscans, who inhabited present-day Italy, built advanced sewage systems and were skilled in bridge and aqueduct construction.

Israelites – Monotheism: The Israelites were among the first groups to practice monotheism, belief in a single god, which influenced religions such as Judaism, Christianity, and Islam.

Carthage – Trade Power: Carthaginians became a major trading power in the Mediterranean, known for their advanced maritime trade and formidable navy.

Assyrians – Military Organization: The Assyrians created an organized army, employing advanced military techniques and diverse formations.

Romans – Law and Engineering: The Romans developed the first cohesive legal system and advanced engineering techniques, including roads, aqueducts, and amphitheaters that have lasted for centuries.

Nubians – Kerma Fortress: The Nubian civilization built powerful fortifications like the Kerma fortress, serving as a defensive stronghold and trade center.

Sumerians – Mathematics and Astronomy: The Sumerians developed a base-60 mathematical system used in astronomy and calculations, forming a foundation for later mathematical achievements.

•Subchapter 4.2: Cultures and Their Lost Cities

Atlantis – The Lost City of Atlantis: The legendary Atlantis, described by Plato, was said to be an advanced civilization that disappeared underwater. Its location remains a mystery and inspires numerous theories and explorations.

Maya – City of Tikal: Tikal, one of the most important Maya cities in present-day Guatemala, was abandoned around the 10th century for unknown reasons, leaving monumental structures in the jungle.

Inca – Machu Picchu: Machu Picchu, high in the Andes, was never discovered by Spanish conquistadors but was abandoned after the fall of the Inca Empire and rediscovered in 1911.

Anasazi – Mesa Verde: The Anasazi, an ancient North American culture, built the cliff settlement of Mesa Verde. The city was abandoned around the 13th century, with reasons remaining unclear.

Egypt – City of Tanis: Tanis was an important city in ancient Egypt that fell into ruin after the New Kingdom. It is known for tombs filled with gold and treasures.

Romans – Pompeii: Pompeii, a Roman city, was destroyed by the eruption of Mount Vesuvius in 79 CE and preserved as a "time capsule" of ancient life.

Persians – Persepolis: Persepolis was the capital of the Persian Empire, famous for its palaces and temples, but was destroyed by Alexander the Great in 330 BCE.

Khmer – Angkor: Angkor, the capital of the Khmer Empire in Cambodia, is one of the largest lost cities, known for monumental temples like Angkor Wat. It was abandoned in the 15th century.

Nabataeans – Petra: Petra, the "city carved in rock" in Jordan, was a Nabataean trade center. It was abandoned after an earthquake in the 4th century CE.

Indus Valley Civilization – Harappa: Harappa and Mohenjo-Daro were key cities of the Indus Valley Civilization, abandoned around 1900 BCE, likely due to climate changes.

Hittites – Hattusa: Hattusa, the capital of the Hittite Empire in modern Turkey, was abandoned in the 12th century BCE due to invasions and destruction.

Olmecs – La Venta: La Venta was a central city of the Olmec civilization, known for colossal stone heads. It declined around 400 BCE, leaving behind mysterious sculptures.

Aksumite Empire – City of Aksum: Aksum was the capital of the Aksumite Empire in modern Ethiopia, dominating trade in the Red Sea region before being abandoned in the 7th century CE.

Greeks – Helike: Helike, a Greek city, sank after an earthquake and tsunami around 373 BCE, possibly inspiring legends of Atlantis.

Mali Empire – Timbuktu: Timbuktu was a cultural and scholarly center in the Mali Empire. Though it still exists, it declined, with many of its treasures and manuscripts lost.

Songhai Empire – Gao: Gao was the capital of the Songhai Empire in West Africa, a hub of gold and salt trade, until its fall to Moroccan invaders in the 16th century.

Celtic City of Alesia: Alesia, a Celtic city that resisted Roman forces under Julius Caesar, was abandoned after the Roman conquest and faded into history.

Maurya Empire – Pataliputra: Pataliputra was the capital of the Maurya Empire in India, famous for its advanced fortifications, but it was abandoned in the 4th century CE.

Aztec Empire – Tenochtitlan: Tenochtitlan, the Aztec capital, was conquered and destroyed by Spanish conquistadors led by Hernán Cortés in 1521.

City of Cahokia: Located in the Mississippi Valley, Cahokia was one of the largest pre-Columbian cities in North America, inhabited by the Mississippian culture until it was abandoned around the 13th century.

•Subchapter 4.3: Famous Battles and Their Mysteries

Battle of Marathon (490 BCE): Despite being outnumbered, the Greeks defeated the Persians at Marathon. One mystery is the Greeks' use of the phalanx formation, which caught the Persians off guard and led to victory.

Battle of Thermopylae (480 BCE): Led by Leonidas, 300 Spartans held off a vast Persian army for three days. The mystery lies in how such a small group managed to fight for so long against overwhelming forces.

Battle of Cannae (216 BCE): Hannibal crushed the Roman army using a double envelopment maneuver. His brilliant plan remains a mystery and marks him as one of history's greatest strategists.

Battle of the Catalaunian Plains (451 CE): Roman forces under Flavius Aetius defeated the Huns. A mystery remains why Attila retreated despite having the chance to continue fighting.

Battle of Hastings (1066): William the Conqueror defeated King Harold II, gaining control of England. The exact sequence of events and why Harold chose a frontal assault remain unclear.

Battle of Grunwald (1410): Polish-Lithuanian forces defeated the Teutonic Knights. Though well-documented, the exact location of the Teutonic camp and their retreat strategy remain unknown.

Siege of Constantinople (1453): The fall of Constantinople ended the Byzantine Empire. The mystery is why Byzantium received so little support from Western states.

Battle of Lepanto (1571): A naval clash between Christian and Ottoman fleets. The mystery is how the smaller Christian fleet managed to defeat the larger Ottoman force.

Battle of Vienna (1683): This battle ended the Ottoman offensive in Europe. The mystery is why Ottoman commander Kara Mustafa failed to prepare adequate defenses, allowing for a Christian counterattack.

Battle of Austerlitz (1805): Napoleon defeated Austrian and Russian forces with a maneuver that remains famous. The mystery is how he anticipated the enemy's movements so accurately.

Battle of Waterloo (1815): Napoleon's defeat marked the end of his rule. One mystery is his decision to begin the battle later than planned, which may have contributed to his loss.

American Civil War – Battle of Gettysburg (1863): A turning point in the Civil War. One mystery is why General Lee opted for a frontal assault instead of an encirclement.

Battle of Gallipoli (1915-1916): The Gallipoli campaign was a costly defeat for the Allies. The mystery lies in why they undertook such a risky operation with chaotic tactics.

Battle of Kursk (1943): The largest tank battle of WWII. It remains a mystery why Hitler launched an attack despite the Soviets being well-prepared.

Normandy Landings (1944): The D-Day invasion was an Allied success, but the details of the surprise attack and why the Germans were caught off guard continue to be studied.

Battle of Midway (1942): The Americans destroyed four Japanese carriers. The mystery is why Japanese commanders made so many planning errors.

Battle of Monte Cassino (1944): Multiple Allied assaults eventually broke through German defenses. The mystery is why Allied commanders chose such brutal, costly assaults.

Battle of Britain (1940): Germany sought air superiority over Britain. Debates continue over why Hitler halted bombing RAF airfields, allowing the British to rebuild.

Battle of Stalingrad (1942-1943): This battle drained German forces on the Eastern Front. The mystery is why Hitler refused to withdraw his troops in a disastrous situation.

Battle of Agincourt (1415): A small English force defeated a much larger French army. The mystery is how the English, with fewer soldiers, managed to crush the French forces.

•Subchapter 4.4: Famous Rulers and Their Secrets

Alexander the Great: The cause of his death at age 32 remains a mystery, with theories ranging from poisoning to illness or exhaustion from relentless campaigns.

Cleopatra VII: Cleopatra, the last queen of Egypt, led a life filled with intrigue and romance, notably with Julius Caesar and Mark Antony. Her death is a mystery—legend says she died from a cobra bite, though this may be myth.

Caesar Augustus: The first emperor of Rome, who preserved the illusion of a republic after seizing power. His secret lay in his ability to maintain control without overt titles.

Nero: Known for his controversial rule, with rumors he set Rome ablaze. His reign's mystery lies in his psychological hold over subjects and his growing instability.

Tutankhamun: The young pharaoh died suddenly at 19. His death remains mysterious, with speculation of genetic illness, accident, or murder.

Charlemagne (Charles the Great): A prominent medieval ruler whose success was rooted in combining politics, military strength, and religious influence to unify Western Europe.

Henry VIII: The famous English king with six wives who changed the state religion. His reign's secret was his determination to secure a male heir, which led to religious and political upheaval in England.

Louis XIV – The Sun King: Known for his grand palace at Versailles, Louis XIV was a master of propaganda. His secret was controlling the nobility through court rituals and carefully crafted image.

Ivan the Terrible: Russia's first tsar, notorious for his brutal rule and the terror-driven Oprichnina. His unpredictable shifts from religious to cruel made him a mystery.

Elizabeth I: The "Virgin Queen" of England, who never married. Her secret was her skill in balancing political rivals and maintaining control over England.

Peter the Great: The Russian tsar who modernized Russia after traveling through Europe incognito to learn new technologies, which enabled him to implement revolutionary reforms.

Napoleon Bonaparte: The Emperor of the French who conquered much of Europe. His success lay in his psychological mastery of warfare, yet the cause of his death on Saint Helena remains mysterious—possibly poisoning.

Catherine the Great: Catherine II took the Russian throne after a coup against her husband. Her secret was skillfully building alliances and enacting reforms to solidify her rule.

Frederick the Great: The Prussian king who transformed his state into a military power. His secret was strict military discipline and expert battlefield tactics.

Maria Theresa: The Habsburg ruler who governed with authority. Her secret was balancing state interests with family alliances, preserving her dynasty's power.

Akbar the Great: The Mughal emperor of India known for religious tolerance. His secret was his ability to integrate diverse cultures and religions, ensuring stable rule over his vast empire.

Franz Joseph I: The Austrian emperor who ruled for 68 years. His secret to long rule was steadfast loyalty to the monarchy, despite personal and political tragedies.

Genghis Khan: Founder of the Mongol Empire, who conquered most of Asia and Eastern Europe. His success lay in his strict laws and ability to unite Mongol tribes into a formidable force.

Haile Selassie: The last emperor of Ethiopia, believed to be a descendant of King Solomon. His secret was the myth of divine ancestry, which reinforced his authority with religious significance.

Saladin: The Muslim ruler who recaptured Jerusalem from the Crusaders. His success lay in a blend of diplomacy, military effectiveness, and tolerance toward conquered Christians.

Subchapter 4.5: Intriguing Inventions and Discoveries

The Wheel (c. 3500 BCE): Invented by the Sumerians in Mesopotamia, the wheel revolutionized transportation and technology and is considered one of the most important inventions in human history.

Papyrus and Paper: The Egyptians created papyrus, the first writing material, while the Chinese invented paper around 100 CE, facilitating the growth of literature and communication.

Edison's Light Bulb (1879): Although earlier work on the light bulb existed, Thomas Edison developed the first practical model, revolutionizing nightlife and industry.

Gutenberg's Printing Press (1450): Johannes Gutenberg's invention of the printing press enabled mass production of books, fostering education and spreading knowledge.

The Compass: Invented in China, the compass made open-sea navigation possible, paving the way for major geographical discoveries and global exploration.

Gunpowder: Invented in China, gunpowder transformed warfare, leading to the development of firearms and artillery.

The Telegraph (1837): Samuel Morse's invention allowed instant long-distance communication, revolutionizing commerce, politics, and international relations.

Smallpox Vaccine (1796): Edward Jenner discovered that smallpox could be prevented by vaccination, initiating the era of modern preventive medicine.

The Steam Engine (17th Century): James Watt's improvements to the steam engine fueled the Industrial Revolution, advancing industry and transportation.

Radioactivity (1896): The discovery of radioactivity by Henri Becquerel and further research by Marie Curie enabled advancements in medicine and nuclear energy.

Penicillin (1928): Alexander Fleming's discovery of penicillin began the antibiotic era, allowing treatment for many previously fatal diseases.

Theory of Relativity (1905–1915): Albert Einstein's theory transformed our understanding of time, space, and gravity, influencing the field of physics.

The Internet (1960s): Initially developed as a military project, the internet became a global medium that transformed communication, commerce, and information access.

Morse Code: Samuel Morse created a system of symbols that allowed for quick telegraphic message transmission, accelerating the development of communication.

3D Printing: 3D printing technology enables the creation of three-dimensional objects from digital models, with applications in medicine, industry, and art.

GPS (1973): The Global Positioning System allows precise worldwide location tracking, essential in navigation, rescue operations, and logistics.

The Airplane (1903): The Wright brothers built the first powered airplane, opening a new era of international travel and aviation development.

The Telephone (1876): Invented by Alexander Graham Bell, the telephone revolutionized communication, allowing instant conversations over long distances.

DNA and the Genetic Code (1953): James Watson and Francis Crick discovered DNA's structure, laying the foundation for genetics and heredity research.

The Laser (1960): The invention of the laser has widespread applications in medicine, telecommunications, scientific research, and military technology.

Chapter 5: Amazing Animals

•Subchapter 5.1: Predators and Their Hunting Strategies

Great White Shark: Great white sharks use a "strike from below" technique, attacking prey such as seals from beneath in a swift, vertical motion that leaves the target little chance to escape.

Lions – Group Hunting: Lions hunt in prides, often surrounding and trapping prey, using the speed and strength of the entire group to increase their success in taking down large animals.

Eagles – Dive from Above: Eagles utilize their sharp eyesight and rapid descent from heights to surprise prey like rabbits and snakes, often grabbing them with powerful talons before they can react.

Orb-Weaving Spiders: These spiders construct intricate webs that act as traps. When an insect gets ensnared, the spider quickly wraps it in silk and injects venom to paralyze it.

Orcas (Killer Whales): Orcas hunt in groups, employing complex strategies like knocking seals off ice floes or herding fish, using sonar to communicate and coordinate attacks.

Hawks – Low-Level Flight: Hawks fly close to the ground, using terrain for cover to surprise prey like rodents and birds, allowing them to strike with great speed.

Praying Mantis – Ambush Predator: The mantis stays motionless, blending into its surroundings until prey comes close, then swiftly grabs it with long forelimbs.

Owls – Silent Flight: Owls have specially shaped feathers that enable silent flight, allowing them to approach prey, like mice and birds, undetected before striking.

Constrictor Snakes (Boas, Pythons): These snakes wrap around their prey and constrict it, tightening their grip with each breath the prey takes until it stops breathing.

Wolves – Endurance Hunting: Wolves are known for their stamina in pursuing prey over long distances, wearing it down until it becomes an easy target.

Leatherback Turtles – Jellyfish Traps: Leatherback turtles hunt jellyfish by swimming around them and carefully gripping the tentacles to avoid stings.

Octopuses – Camouflage and Surprise: Octopuses can change their skin color and texture to blend in, then suddenly extend their arms to capture prey like crabs or fish.

Leopards – Stealth and Quick Attack: Leopards hunt alone, stalking prey quietly before launching a swift attack. They can also drag their kill up a tree to protect it from other predators.

Hammerhead Sharks: Hammerhead sharks hunt stingrays by pinning them to the ocean floor with their broad heads, immobilizing prey for an easy attack.

Sperm Whales: Sperm whales hunt squid in the deep ocean, using echolocation to locate prey in the dark depths.

Cheetahs – Speed for Short Distances: Cheetahs are the fastest land animals, reaching speeds of up to 120 km/h (75 mph) in short bursts, ambushing prey with a quick, surprise attack.

Army Ants: These ants hunt in large groups, forming "armies" that sweep through an area, attacking any animals in their path.

Crocodiles – Water-Based Ambush: Crocodiles lie in wait underwater, springing out when an animal approaches the shore, dragging prey into the water with immense force.

Bald Eagle: The bald eagle swoops down to catch fish, pulling them from the water with strong talons. They can also snatch prey from other birds.

Pumas – Silent Approach: Pumas hunt by stalking prey quietly, then leaping with powerful force, making them highly effective predators in mountainous and forested areas.

•Subchapter 5.2: The Oldest and Smallest Species

Greenland Shark (Oldest Vertebrate): Greenland sharks can live up to 400 years, with their longevity attributed to a slow metabolism and the cold temperatures of their oceanic habitat.

Turritopsis dohrnii ("Immortal Jellyfish"): This jellyfish can revert to its polyp stage, essentially reversing its life cycle, giving it a potential for biological "immortality."

Reef Sponges (Oldest Multicellular Organisms): Sponges are among the oldest organisms on Earth, dating back about 760 million years, and have remained largely unchanged.

Coelacanth (Living Fossil): The coelacanth fish was thought extinct for 65 million years until rediscovered in the 20th century, earning it the title of a "living fossil."

Sturgeon (Water Dinosaurs): Sturgeons have existed for over 200 million years and have retained many prehistoric characteristics.

Cockroaches (Indestructible Survivors): Cockroaches, dating back 320 million years, are highly resilient and can survive in extreme conditions.

Giant Tortoise (Long-Lived Reptile): Giant tortoises from the Galapagos and Seychelles can live over 150 years, making them some of the longest-living animals on Earth.

Ants and Termites (Ancient Societies): Ants and termites have thrived for around 100 million years, maintaining social structures that support their survival.

Planaria (Tiny Yet Resilient): These small flatworms can regenerate entire bodies from fragments, demonstrating extraordinary adaptability.

Horseshoe Crab (Living Relic): The horseshoe crab, resembling ancient trilobites, has existed for about 450 million years, making it one of the oldest living species.

Arctic Tern (Long-Distance Bird): This small bird undertakes the longest migration of any species, covering up to 71,000 kilometers yearly between the Arctic and Antarctic.

Paedocypris Fish: Among the world's smallest vertebrates, reaching only 8 mm in length, this fish inhabits acidic peat swamps in Southeast Asia.

Amoebas (Single-Celled Survivors): Amoebas are some of the oldest life forms, existing for billions of years and thriving in a variety of environments.

Tardigrades (Water Bears): These microscopic animals can survive extreme conditions, from intense heat to the vacuum of space, dating back around 500 million years.

Cymothoa exigua ("Parasitic Tongue"): This parasite replaces the tongue of a fish with its own body, making it one of the most unique and eerie adaptations in nature.

Ostracods (Tiny Shells): These tiny marine organisms, with ancestors dating back around 480 million years, are among the oldest marine species.

Monte Iberia Eleuth Frog: One of the smallest frogs in the world, measuring just 8–9 mm, found only in Cuba.

Polychaetes (Marine Annelids): These segmented worms have lived on the ocean floor for about 500 million years, enduring countless climate and geological shifts.

Scarlet Crabs (Small but Adaptable): These tiny crabs, a few millimeters long, inhabit tropical beaches, thriving in extremely hot environments.

Corals (Ancient Reef Builders): Coral reefs are created by microscopic organisms that have existed for hundreds of millions of years, with some reefs predating human civilization.

•Subchapter 5.3: Animal Records and Oddities

Giraffe – Tallest Land Animal: Giraffes reach up to 5.5 meters (18 feet) in height, making them the tallest land animals. Their long necks allow them to reach leaves other herbivores cannot.

Blue Whale – Largest Animal on Earth: The blue whale, reaching up to 30 meters (98 feet) and weighing as much as 180 tons, is the largest animal ever known to exist.

Bee Hummingbird – Smallest Bird: The bee hummingbird is the world's smallest bird, measuring only 5 cm (2 inches) in length and weighing about 2 grams.

Cheetah – Fastest Runner: Cheetahs can sprint up to 120 km/h (75 mph) over short distances, making them the fastest land mammals.

Atlas Moth – Largest Wingspan among Insects: The atlas moth has the largest wingspan of any insect, reaching up to 30 cm (12 inches).

Water Deer – "Vampire Deer": This unique deer species, found in China and Korea, has long canine teeth that resemble vampire fangs.

Muntjac (Barking Deer): Known as the "barking deer," muntjacs make a call that sounds like a bark, which serves to deter predators.

Pufferfish – "Balloon" Defense Strategy: This fish inflates itself to appear larger, using spines on its body to scare off predators.

Rabbits – Extreme Breeding: Rabbits have impressive reproductive abilities, with females capable of producing up to 12 litters per year.

Cockroach – Surviving Without a Head: Cockroaches can live without their heads for a week, eventually dying of starvation due to their simple circulatory system.

Japanese Firefly Squid – Unique Green Light: The Japanese firefly squid emits green light, an unusual phenomenon among light-producing animals.

Fire Ants – Living Rafts: Fire ants form "living rafts" with their bodies during floods, allowing the colony to float and survive on water surfaces.

Coconut Crab – Strongest Claws: The coconut crab has the strongest claws relative to body weight, capable of cracking open coconuts.

Hagfish – Slime Defense: Hagfish produce large amounts of slime to deter predators, often clogging the mouth of any attacker that tries to eat them.

Aye-Aye Lemur – Humanlike Eyes: Aye-ayes have large, round eyes, giving them a "human" appearance that aids their night vision.

Chameleon – Independently Moving Eyes: Chameleons can move each eye independently, allowing them to watch two directions at once.

African Elephant – Largest Land Brain: African elephants have the largest brains of any land animal, supporting their advanced social skills and impressive memory.

Cabbage Whitefly – Longest-Lived Insect: The cabbage whitefly has an exceptionally long lifespan for an insect, living up to 20 years.

Naked Mole Rat – Longest-Lived Rodent: Native to Africa, the naked mole rat can live up to 30 years, an unusually long lifespan for a rodent.

Argentine Lake Duck – Spiral Reproductive Organ: This duck species has a unique spiral-shaped reproductive organ, the only known instance in the bird world, which enhances its reproductive success.

•Subchapter 5.4: Animals and Their Intelligence

Bottlenose Dolphins: Dolphins demonstrate problem-solving skills, communicate through complex vocalizations, and even recognize themselves in mirrors, indicating self-awareness.

Chimpanzees: Chimpanzees create and use tools to access food and learn through imitation. They show advanced social and emotional intelligence, mirroring human behaviors.

African Grey Parrots: Known for their ability to mimic human speech, African grey parrots understand words, count, and distinguish colors, ranking them among the most intelligent birds.

African Elephants: Elephants have excellent memories, the ability to plan, and can use tools. They also show empathy and care for sick members of their herd.

Corvids (Crows, Rooks, and Ravens): Corvids are known for their intelligence—they use tools, solve complex puzzles, and remember food storage locations.

Octopuses: With a highly developed nervous system, octopuses exhibit memory, problem-solving skills, and object manipulation, making them exceptionally intelligent invertebrates.

Dogs: Dogs can learn commands, recognize human and animal emotions, and retain a large vocabulary. Breeds like border collies excel in problem-solving tasks.

Rats: Known for their learning and adaptability, rats navigate mazes, recognize patterns, and learn based on rewards and punishments.

Ants: Although individually simple, ants display collective intelligence within colonies, creating communication networks and making joint decisions.

Kea Parrots: These New Zealand parrots solve intricate puzzles and show curiosity and a propensity for experimentation.

Capuchin Monkeys: Capuchins use tools, like stones to crack nuts, and display complex social behaviors and communication skills.

Orcas (Killer Whales): Orcas hunt in groups, using sophisticated hunting strategies, and can mimic the sounds of other animals, indicating high social intelligence.

Lions: Lions show complex social behaviors and collaborative hunting tactics, highlighting their intelligence in planning and strategy.

Honeybees: Bees communicate through the "waggle dance," which conveys information about nectar sources, a complex communication system among insects.

Wild Boars: Boars are adept at problem-solving and learning from others, allowing them to avoid traps and locate food more efficiently.

Owls: With developed hunting skills and strong spatial memory, owls can locate and remember object positions. Their silent flight and camouflage also demonstrate high adaptability.

Humboldt Squid: These squid communicate and camouflage through skin color changes, requiring coordination and rapid information processing.

Bonobos: Closely related to chimpanzees, bonobos show advanced social skills, such as cooperation, conflict resolution, and empathy.

Pigeons: Known for excellent spatial memory and pattern recognition, pigeons were historically used to carry messages, showcasing their cognitive abilities.

Meerkats: Living in social groups, meerkats display sophisticated protective behaviors, such as appointing sentries who warn the group of danger, reflecting strong communication and organizational skills.

•Subchapter 5.5: Unusual Symbioses and Adaptations

Coral and Algae (Coral Symbiosis): Corals live in symbiosis with microscopic algae (zooxanthellae), which provide energy through photosynthesis in exchange for shelter. This partnership is essential to coral reef formation.

Ants and Aphids: Ants tend to aphids, protecting them from predators in return for a sweet secretion called honeydew produced by the aphids.

Blind Cave Creatures and Symbiotic Fish: In caves, blind creatures coexist with limited-vision fish—both have adapted to darkness and use mutual signals to navigate safely.

Pilot Fish and Sharks: Pilot fish often accompany sharks, feeding on their parasites and leftover food, benefiting both species.

Fungi and Plants – Mycorrhiza: Fungi connect with plant roots, providing minerals while receiving sugars from the plants' photosynthesis process.

Oxpecker Birds and Buffalo: Oxpecker birds sit on large mammals like buffalo, eating parasites off their skin and providing pest control for their hosts.

Sailfish and Cephalopods: Sailfish sometimes cooperate with smaller cephalopods to distract predators, aiding both in defense.

Hermit Crabs and Sea Anemones: Hermit crabs attach sea anemones to their shells for protection, benefiting from their stinging cells while the anemones gain mobility and new food sources.

Parasitic Wasps and Caterpillars: Wasps lay eggs in caterpillars, which serve as hosts for the wasp larvae, although it's fatal for the caterpillars.

Pistol Shrimp and Goby Fish: Pistol shrimp and goby fish share a burrow, with the goby acting as a lookout while the shrimp provides shelter.

Bacteria in Ruminants' Stomachs: Ruminants, like cows, work with bacteria in their stomachs that help digest cellulose, enabling them to break down plant fibers.

Orchid Mantis and Flowers: Orchid mantises resemble orchids, allowing them to ambush prey while blending in, taking advantage of their disguise.

Cuttlefish and Bioluminescent Bacteria: Cuttlefish host glowing bacteria, which help them blend into moonlight, making them invisible to predators.

Fasciola Gigantica and Aquatic Insects (Behavior Manipulation): These parasites manipulate hosts to stay near water surfaces, making them easy prey and allowing the parasites to transfer to new hosts.

Egyptian Plover and Crocodiles: The plover bird eats food scraps and parasites from a crocodile's mouth, helping keep the crocodile's teeth healthy.

Eucalyptus and Koalas (Specialized Diet): Koalas feed almost exclusively on eucalyptus leaves, which are toxic to most animals, giving them access to a unique food source.

Owls and Harriers (Hunting Cooperation): Some owl species cooperate with harriers, which locate bird nests; owls then consume leftover prey, forming a unique hunting relationship.

Lantern Fish and Algae: Lantern fish house bioluminescent algae that attract prey and mask the fish from predators by emitting "camouflaging" light.

Alpine Edelweiss and Rock Rose: Edelweiss produces chemicals that inhibit the growth of other plants, allowing it to thrive in challenging mountain environments.

Grasslands and Nitrogen-Fixing Bacteria: Meadow plants partner with bacteria that fix atmospheric nitrogen, enriching the soil and supporting better plant growth.

Chapter 6: People Who Changed the World

•Subchapter 6.1: Inventors and Their Breakthroughs

Nikola Tesla – Alternating Current (AC): Tesla developed the AC power system, which revolutionized long-distance energy transmission and laid the foundation for modern electrical grids.

Thomas Edison – Light Bulb and Phonograph: Edison invented the light bulb, enabling lighting in homes and public spaces, and the phonograph, the first device for recording sound.

Johannes Gutenberg – Printing Press: Gutenberg created the first printing press, allowing for mass book production and the widespread dissemination of knowledge, sparking an educational revolution.

James Watt – Improved Steam Engine: Watt developed a more efficient steam engine that powered the Industrial Revolution, advancing transport and manufacturing.

Alexander Graham Bell – Telephone: Bell invented the telephone, revolutionizing communication by allowing real-time conversations over long distances.

Marie Curie – Radioactivity: Curie discovered the elements polonium and radium, and her research on radioactivity became foundational in modern physics and nuclear medicine.

Henry Ford – Assembly Line: Ford introduced the assembly line in car manufacturing, revolutionizing industry by reducing production costs and making cars affordable for the masses.

Wright Brothers – Aviation: The Wright brothers built the first powered airplane, opening a new era of international travel and air transport.

Albert Einstein – Theory of Relativity: Einstein's theory of relativity transformed science's understanding of space, time, and gravity, deeply impacting physics.

Steve Jobs – Smartphones and Personal Computers: As a co-founder of Apple, Jobs pioneered personal computing technology and introduced products that changed communication and work globally.

Tim Berners-Lee – World Wide Web: Berners-Lee created the World Wide Web, making global information accessible and transforming the internet into a universal communication medium.

George Washington Carver – Crop Science: Carver developed numerous uses for crops like peanuts, which greatly impacted both agriculture and the economy.

Guglielmo Marconi – Radio: Marconi developed radio technology, enabling wireless communication and revolutionizing information sharing.

Leonardo da Vinci – Inventions and Art: Da Vinci designed early prototypes of flying machines, submarines, and other inventions, advancing technology centuries ahead of his time.

Alessandro Volta – Battery: Volta invented the first electric battery, marking a milestone in energy technology and enabling portable power sources.

John Logie Baird – Television: Baird demonstrated the first television system for transmitting images, revolutionizing media and information access.

Samuel Morse – Telegraph and Morse Code: Morse created the telegraph and a code for it, allowing fast communication over long distances before the advent of the telephone.

Elon Musk – Space and Energy Innovations: Musk founded companies such as Tesla and SpaceX, pioneering eco-friendly technology and space exploration, transforming modern transportation.

Louis Pasteur – Vaccines and Microbiology: Pasteur discovered pasteurization and developed vaccines, greatly impacting medical science and public health.

Niklaus Wirth – Programming Language: Wirth created the Pascal programming language, foundational in teaching programming and advancing computer science.

•Subchapter 6.2: The Greatest Scientific Minds

Albert Einstein: A pioneer in theoretical physics and the theory of relativity, Einstein revolutionized the understanding of time, space, and gravity, impacting the development of technologies like GPS.

Isaac Newton: Developed the laws of motion and universal gravitation, which became the foundation of modern physics and mathematics, particularly in calculus.

Galileo Galilei: Led a revolution in astronomy, confirming the heliocentric model of the solar system and refining the telescope for more accurate observations of space.

Marie Curie: A pioneer in radioactivity research, she was awarded two Nobel Prizes for discovering polonium and radium, opening pathways for nuclear medicine and energy.

Charles Darwin: Created the theory of evolution through natural selection, transforming the understanding of species origins and the development of life on Earth.

Nikola Tesla: Invented alternating current (AC), electrical generators, and numerous innovations that shaped energy technology and wireless power transmission.

Richard Feynman: Advanced quantum physics and quantum electrodynamics, deepening the understanding of particle interactions and bringing new applications in electronics and technology.

Aristotle: Established foundational principles across many sciences, including biology, logic, and physics; his systematic approach laid the groundwork for centuries of scientific advancement.

James Clerk Maxwell: Formulated the theory of electromagnetism, uniting electricity, magnetism, and light, which became a cornerstone of modern physics.

Stephen Hawking: His research on black holes and cosmology, particularly Hawking radiation, bridged quantum mechanics with general relativity.

Michael Faraday: Discovered electromagnetic induction, enabling the development of electric power generation and forming the basis of modern electronics.

Gregor Mendel: Known as the father of genetics, Mendel's research on trait inheritance in plants established the foundations of modern genetics.

Leonhard Euler: A prolific mathematician whose contributions to calculus, number theory, geometry, and mechanics led to numerous equations and formulas that remain essential.

Enrico Fermi: A nuclear physics pioneer who built the first nuclear reactor; his work on atomic fission launched the atomic age.

Niels Bohr: Developed the Bohr model of the atom and made key contributions to quantum mechanics, fundamental for molecular physics and atomic theory.

Johannes Kepler: Formulated the laws of planetary motion, foundational to astronomy and a confirmation of Copernicus's heliocentric model.

Rosalind Franklin: Her research on DNA structure led to the discovery of the double helix, profoundly impacting molecular biology and genetics.

Erwin Schrödinger: Developed the Schrödinger equation, fundamental in quantum mechanics for describing quantum states of particles.

Alan Turing: Regarded as the father of computer science, he created the concept of the Turing machine, laying the foundation for modern computing and artificial intelligence.

Carl Linnaeus: The father of biological taxonomy, Linnaeus introduced species classification, facilitating the study and categorization of Earth's biodiversity.

•Subchapter 6.3: Visionary Artists and Their Works

Leonardo da Vinci – Mona Lisa and The Last Supper: His works are characterized by perfection of detail and innovative use of chiaroscuro. Mona Lisa is famed for her enigmatic smile, and The Last Supper stands as one of the most important fresco compositions.

Michelangelo Buonarroti – Frescoes in the Sistine Chapel and David: His Sistine Chapel frescoes, especially The Creation of Adam, captivate with their detail and dynamism, and his sculpture David symbolizes Renaissance excellence.

Vincent van Gogh – Starry Night: Known for his expressive use of color and brushstroke movement, Van Gogh's Starry Night is filled with emotion and dynamism, becoming an icon of expressionism.

Pablo Picasso – Guernica: This monumental piece on war and suffering demonstrates the power of abstract forms to convey intense emotion and expression.

Salvador Dalí – The Persistence of Memory: The surreal clocks in this painting symbolize the transience of time and the irrationality of dreams, becoming emblematic of surrealism.

Frida Kahlo – The Two Fridas: Kahlo mastered autobiographical symbolism. The Two Fridas reflects her dual identity and internal struggles.

Rembrandt van Rijn – The Night Watch: Rembrandt used light and shadow to convey emotions and the hierarchy of figures in this grand group composition.

Claude Monet – Water Lilies: A pioneer of impressionism, Monet's Water Lilies captures subtle shifts in light and color on the water's surface, redefining landscape art.

Gustav Klimt – The Kiss: Klimt fused gold, color, and ornamentation in The Kiss, a symbol of love and passion, making it one of the most recognized works of Art Nouveau.

Edvard Munch – The Scream: This painting expresses fear and alienation, and the figure in The Scream has become an emblem of existential anxiety.

Andy Warhol – Marilyn Monroe and Campbell's Soup Cans: Representing pop art, Warhol transformed everyday objects into art, redefining the boundaries of popular culture.

Georgia O'Keeffe – White Lilies: Her magnified flower paintings revolutionized floral art and contributed to the growth of American abstract art.

Henri Matisse – The Dance: Matisse used simplified forms and intense colors to express movement and joy, establishing him as a master of Fauvism.

Jackson Pollock – No. 5, 1948: Pollock's groundbreaking "drip painting" technique captured spontaneity and emotion through abstract paint pouring.

Caravaggio – The Supper at Emmaus: Caravaggio introduced realism and sharp contrasts of light and shadow, infusing drama into religious and historical scenes.

René Magritte – The Son of Man: The face obscured by an apple in this work inspired a surreal exploration of identity and perception of reality.

Antoni Gaudí – Sagrada Familia: Gaudí merged architecture and art in this monumental cathedral in Barcelona, full of fantastical forms inspired by nature.

Hieronymus Bosch – The Garden of Earthly Delights: Bosch crafted surreal, detailed visions reflecting both the sinfulness and spirituality of humanity.

Marcel Duchamp – Fountain: By exhibiting a urinal as "art," Duchamp revolutionized conceptualism and raised questions about the essence of art.

Kazimir Malevich – Black Square: Malevich's Black Square was a

•Subchapter 6.4: Pioneers of Exploration and Discovery

Christopher Columbus: In 1492, Columbus embarked on a voyage that led to the discovery of the Americas by Europeans, opening the door to the colonization of the New World.

Marco Polo: In the 13th century, Marco Polo traveled to China, documenting the culture and wealth of Asia in his Book of the Marvels of the World, sparking European interest in Eastern lands.

Vasco da Gama: The Portuguese navigator reached India by sea in 1498, establishing a new trade route to Asia and revolutionizing intercontinental commerce.

Ferdinand Magellan: He led the first expedition to circumnavigate the Earth (1519–1522), proving the planet's roundness and laying the groundwork for future global exploration.

James Cook: The British explorer mapped the Pacific, discovering Australia, Hawaii, and New Zealand, significantly expanding Europe's geographic knowledge.

Roald Amundsen: The Norwegian polar explorer was the first person to reach the South Pole in 1911, breaking through extreme environmental barriers.

Neil Armstrong: In 1969, Armstrong became the first human to set foot on the Moon, marking a milestone in space exploration.

Amerigo Vespucci: The Italian navigator was the first to recognize that the lands Columbus discovered were part of a new continent, which was subsequently named America in his honor.

Hernán Cortés: The Spanish conquistador conquered the Aztec Empire in 1521, bringing Central America into the European sphere.

Erik the Red: The Viking explorer was the first European to reach Greenland, and his son, Leif Erikson, continued westward, reaching North America.

Zheng He: The Chinese admiral led seven major expeditions westward in the 15th century, expanding Chinese influence and discovering numerous new lands.

Ibn Battuta: The great Muslim traveler journeyed through Africa, the Middle East, Asia, and Europe, documenting cultures and customs across many lands.

David Livingstone: The British explorer of Africa discovered the Victoria Falls and contributed significantly to European exploration of the continent.

Lewis and Clark: Meriwether Lewis and William Clark mapped the western United States from 1804 to 1806, making contact with Indigenous tribes and documenting new territories.

Jacques Cousteau: The ocean explorer popularized underwater exploration and invented the scuba, advancing diving and oceanographic research.

Edmund Hillary and Tenzing Norgay: In 1953, Hillary and Norgay became the first to summit Mount Everest, symbolizing human endurance and determination.

Fridtjof Nansen: The Norwegian polar explorer attempted to reach the North Pole, expanding knowledge about the Arctic and cold regions of the planet.

Robert Peary: The American explorer claimed to be the first to reach the North Pole in 1909, though his achievement remains debated.

Alexander von Humboldt: The German naturalist explored South America, discovering new species and documenting geographical phenomena, influencing the field of ecology.

Jean-François Champollion: The scholar who first deciphered the Rosetta Stone's hieroglyphics, opening the door to understanding ancient Egyptian history.

•Subchapter 6.5: Revolutionaries and Their Ideas

Mahatma Gandhi – Peaceful Resistance and Nonviolence: Gandhi led India's independence movement through principles of peaceful resistance and nonviolence, inspiring movements worldwide.

Martin Luther King Jr. – Racial Equality and Civil Rights: King fought for the rights of African Americans in the U.S., advocating equality and peace, symbolized by his famous "I Have a Dream" speech.

Karl Marx – Socialism and Communism: Marx developed the theory of class struggle and envisioned a classless society, laying the foundation for socialist and communist movements globally.

Thomas Paine – Democratic Ideas and Human Rights: Paine supported American independence and democratic ideals through Common Sense, inspiring freedom movements.

Simón Bolívar – Liberation of Latin America: Bolívar was a key figure in South America's struggle for independence from Spain, inspiring ideas of unity with his vision of a "Gran Colombia."

Emmeline Pankhurst – Suffrage Movement: The British suffragist fought for women's voting rights, using radical methods that transformed the role of women in society.

Vladimir Lenin – October Revolution and Marxism-Leninism: Lenin led the Bolshevik Revolution in Russia, establishing a communist state founded on Marxism.

Che Guevara – Anti-Imperialism Movement: Guevara, a revolutionary icon in Latin America, fought against imperialism and championed socialism, inspiring leftist movements worldwide.

Nelson Mandela – Fight Against Apartheid: Mandela symbolized the struggle against racial segregation in South Africa and promoted national reconciliation after the end of apartheid.

Rosa Luxemburg – Radical Democracy and Workers' Revolution: A co-founder of the German Communist Party, Luxemburg advocated for worker-led governance and social revolution.

Mustafa Kemal Atatürk – Modernization and Secularism: Atatürk transformed Turkey into a secular, modern state, introducing reforms that revolutionized Turkish society.

Fidel Castro – Cuban Revolution and Independence from the U.S.: Castro led the Cuban Revolution, overthrowing the Batista regime and establishing a socialist state free from U.S. influence.

Malcolm X – African American Self-Determination: Malcolm X advocated for the rights of African Americans, emphasizing self-determination and self-defense, contrasting with more peaceful strategies.

Jean-Jacques Rousseau – Ideas of Freedom and the Social Contract: Rousseau's theories on popular sovereignty and the social contract deeply influenced democratic revolutions, especially the French Revolution.

Susan B. Anthony – Women's Rights: A leader in the American suffragist movement, Anthony fought for women's voting rights, impacting civil rights legislation.

Mao Zedong – Cultural Revolution and Communist Ideas: Mao led the Chinese Revolution, establishing communism and implementing radical social reforms that reshaped Chinese society.

Cesar Chavez – Farm Workers' Rights: Chavez organized strikes and campaigns, advocating for better working conditions for farm laborers in the U.S., mainly of Latino descent.

Kwame Nkrumah – African Decolonization: Nkrumah, the first president of Ghana, fought for African colonies' independence, inspiring liberation movements across the continent.

Florence Nightingale – Healthcare Revolution: Nightingale transformed nursing into a professional field, introducing hygiene standards that saved the lives of soldiers and civilians.

Václav Havel – Civil Rights and Freedom of Speech: Havel, a writer and president of Czechoslovakia, led the Velvet Revolution, which brought democracy to the country.

Chapter 7: Culture and Civilization

•Subchapter 7.1: Extraordinary Traditions and Rituals

Naghol (Land Diving) on Vanuatu: Men from the Bunlap tribe perform ritual dives from wooden towers, with vines tied to their ankles, to ensure prosperity and a bountiful harvest.

Holi Festival in India: Participants throw colorful powders, celebrating joy, love, and the triumph of good over evil. This is one of India's most vibrant and joyful festivals.

Día de los Muertos in Mexico: Families honor deceased loved ones by decorating altars with sugar skulls and marigolds, creating a colorful atmosphere to celebrate their memory.

Fire Dancing in Thailand (Loi Krathong): People release lanterns into the water, asking for forgiveness and release from past misdeeds.

Long Neck Ceremony of the Padaung Women (Myanmar): Women wear metal rings around their necks, gradually elongating them as a symbol of beauty and status.

Fire Jumping during Nowruz in Iran: Iranians jump over fires to drive away bad spirits and purify themselves in preparation for the Persian New Year.

Kanamara Matsuri in Japan – Festival of the Phallus: Participants celebrate fertility and health by parading with large symbolic sculptures, rooted in beliefs of protection against sexually transmitted diseases.

Manene Death Ritual in Indonesia: The Toraja people in Indonesia exhume the bodies of their ancestors, dress them, and rebury them, believing that their spirits remain close to family.

Sati – Ancient Indian Funeral Ritual: In this controversial practice, widows would sacrifice themselves on their husband's funeral pyres. Today, it is outlawed.

Sufi Whirling Ritual in Turkey: Dervishes whirl in long, white robes as a form of meditation and prayer, seeking closeness to the divine.

Semana Santa (Holy Week) in Spain: Processions with images of Christ and the Virgin Mary take to the streets, with participants dressed in traditional robes, often with pointed hoods of penance.

Dropping Babies from Heights in India: In some parts of India, babies are safely dropped from heights, such as towers, onto spread blankets, in hopes of bringing luck and health.

La Tomatina in Spain: Participants throw tomatoes at each other in the streets of Buñol, creating a colorful and energetic spectacle.

Barong Masked Ritual in Indonesia: Dancers dressed as Barong, the lion-dragon, perform a dance symbolizing the battle between good and evil to drive away malevolent spirits.

Eidskole Festival in Ethiopia – "Test of Manhood": Young men leap over a line of bulls, symbolizing their transition to adulthood.

Saint George's Day in Bulgaria – Lamb Sacrifice: A lamb is sacrificed in a ritual meant to ensure prosperity and well-being for the family.

Hevehe Shrimp Ritual in Papua New Guinea: Communities perform ritual dances in giant masks to honor ancestral spirits and gain their protection.

Yar Phat – Monkey Festival in Thailand: Monkeys in Lopburi are given a grand feast of fruits and food to show gratitude for their friendship and protection.

Mursi Lip Plate Ritual in Ethiopia: Women from the Mursi tribe insert ceramic plates into their lower lips, representing beauty and status.

Korowai Tribe in New Guinea – Ritualistic Cannibalism: The Korowai practice cannibalism as a spiritual rite of uniting with the deceased, though this tradition is fading due to modern influences.

•Subchapter 7.2: The Strangest Religions and Beliefs

Cargo Cult on the Pacific Islands: Formed after contact with foreign supply shipments ("cargo"), this belief system includes building airstrips and wooden airplanes in hopes of the divine return of "providers" who brought goods.

Church of Maradona in Argentina: A religion created by fans of soccer player Diego Maradona, where he is worshiped as a deity. His birthday is celebrated as a holiday, and his famous "Hand of God" goal has become a symbol of faith.

Raelianism – The UFO Cult: Raelians believe that life on Earth was created by extraterrestrials called the Elohim. Their beliefs mix science and mysticism, with a primary goal of welcoming the return of the Elohim.

Pastafarianism – Church of the Flying Spaghetti Monster: A parody religion created in response to the teaching of creationism. Followers believe that the universe was created by the Flying Spaghetti Monster and wear colanders on their heads.

Church of the SubGenius: A satirical movement mocking organized religion and consumerism, with its "prophet" J.R. "Bob" Dobbs. Followers believe in salvation through laziness.

John Frum Cult on Vanuatu: Followers believe that an American soldier named John Frum will return to the island, bringing prosperity. His day is celebrated annually in anticipation of his return.

Fox Worship (Inari) in Japan: In Japan, the Inari fox spirits are worshiped as deities of fertility, rice, and industry. Ritual offerings are made to bring good fortune in business.

Cao Dai in Vietnam: A syncretic religion that blends elements of Christianity, Buddhism, Taoism, and Islam, worshiping a single god, with richly decorated temples featuring symbols from multiple religions.

Aghori – The Cannibal Sect in India: This ascetic Hindu sect believes that consuming human remains brings enlightenment and liberation from the cycle of reincarnation.

Tiwi Moon Cult in Australia: The Tiwi people believe that the Moon is a deity, and eclipses are caused by spirits attempting to consume it. Rituals are performed to protect the Moon from destruction.

Tenrikyo in Japan: Founded by Miki Nakayama, Tenrikyo teaches that God created humans for joy. Its goal is to achieve a state of joy through love and compassion.

Santo Daime in Brazil: This religion involves the ritual consumption of ayahuasca, a hallucinogenic plant, allowing followers to connect with spirits and reach enlightenment.

Jediism – Faith in the Force: Inspired by Star Wars, Jediism believes in a universal "Force," drawing moral guidance from Jedi characters as a model for ethical living.

Taiping in China: In the 19th century, Hong Xiuquan, who believed himself to be Jesus' brother, led the Taiping Rebellion and founded a religion based on Christianity and his own revelations.

Manichaeism: Founded by the prophet Mani, Manichaeism preached a dualism of good and evil and cycles of rebirth, blending Christianity, Buddhism, and Zoroastrianism.

Zalmoxianism – Dacian Cult in Romania: Zalmoxis, worshiped by the ancient Dacians, is revived by some modern Romanians who perform rituals honoring him, believing he brings spiritual rebirth.

Heaven's Gate – Cosmic Awakening Cult: Followers believed aliens would come to take them to a "heavenly kingdom." This belief tragically ended in a mass suicide among its members.

Sant Mat – The Cult of Light and Sound: A faith movement that emphasizes meditative practices intended to bring enlightenment and direct contact with spiritual energy.

Rastafari Movement in Jamaica: Rastafarians believe that Emperor Haile Selassie I of Ethiopia was a divine incarnation and prophet. They advocate for living in harmony with nature and spiritual freedom.

Broederbond in South Africa: Associated with apartheid ideology, this group combined religious ideas with nationalism, believing God chose Afrikaners to lead South Africa.

•Subchapter 7.3: World Cuisines and Their Specialties

Italy – Neapolitan Pizza: Traditional pizza with a thin, crispy crust, topped with San Marzano tomatoes, mozzarella, and basil. It's one of the most famous dishes worldwide.

Japan – Sushi: Delicate bites of vinegar-seasoned rice served with raw fish, vegetables, and seafood, embodying the essence of Japanese culinary culture.

France – Croissant: Buttery, golden croissants, often enjoyed for breakfast, are a staple of French patisserie and a symbol of culinary elegance in simplicity.

Mexico – Tacos: Corn or flour tortillas filled with meats, beans, cheese, vegetables, and salsa. Tacos are a cornerstone of Mexican cuisine and come in many regional varieties.

India – Curry: Aromatic dishes with meat or vegetables in a spice-based sauce featuring turmeric, cumin, and cardamom. Every region of India has unique curry varieties.

Spain – Paella: A traditional dish from Valencia made with rice, saffron, seafood, chicken, or rabbit, and cooked in a large, shallow pan.

China – Dim Sum Dumplings: Small, steamed or fried dumplings filled with meats, shrimp, or vegetables, often served as a morning or afternoon meal.

Greece – Moussaka: A layered casserole with eggplant, minced meat (often lamb), tomatoes, and béchamel sauce, representing Greek cuisine at its finest.

Turkey – Kebab: Various forms of spit-roasted meats, served with vegetables and pita bread. Kebabs have become popular around the world.

Peru – Ceviche: Raw fish marinated in lime juice with onions, chili peppers, and cilantro. Ceviche is a flagship dish of Peruvian cuisine.

Thailand – Pad Thai: Stir-fried rice noodles with egg, tofu, shrimp, peanuts, and bean sprouts, a hallmark of Thai street food.

Lebanon – Falafel: Fried chickpea or fava bean balls, seasoned with spices, served in pita or on a plate with various accompaniments, a staple of Middle Eastern cuisine.

Ethiopia – Injera: A tangy, spongy flatbread served with various stews and sauces, eaten by hand.

Russia – Borscht: A hearty beet soup often served with sour cream and bread, popular in Russia and Eastern Europe.

Korea – Kimchi: Fermented cabbage and vegetables, seasoned with spicy flavors, a Korean culinary staple known for its health benefits.

Morocco – Tagine: A slow-cooked stew of meat (often lamb), vegetables, dried fruits, and spices, prepared in the clay pot of the same name, which imparts unique flavor.

Nigeria – Jollof Rice: Spicy rice cooked with tomatoes, onions, peppers, and spices. Jollof is a West African staple with various regional adaptations.

USA – Burger: A juicy meat patty on a bun with cheese, vegetables, and condiments, an icon of American fast food.

Poland – Pierogi: Dumplings filled with meat, cheese, cabbage, or fruits, either boiled or fried. Pierogi are a hallmark of Polish cuisine.

Sweden – Köttbullar (Meatballs): Fried meatballs served with potatoes, gravy, and often lingonberry sauce, popularized as a symbol of Swedish home cooking.

Subchapter 7.4: Dances, Art, and Music of Different Cultures

Flamenco Dance (Spain): A passionate dance from Andalusia combining rhythmic clapping, intense body movements, and guitar music. Flamenco expresses emotions such as love, sadness, and passion.

Ukiyo-e Art (Japan): Japanese woodblock prints depicting landscapes, daily life, and portraits of geishas. Ukiyo-e greatly influenced the development of Impressionism.

Hula Dance (Hawaii): A traditional dance with expressive body and hand movements that tell stories about Hawaiian gods, love, and nature. Hula serves as both prayer and cultural expression.

Djembe Drums (West Africa): Percussion instruments used in ritual dances and ceremonies in West Africa. The djembe provides the heartbeat of traditional tribal music and dance.

Classical Ballet (Europe): A dance style from France and Russia known for its elegance and precision, serving as the foundation of modern dance and theatrical arts.

Totem Sculptures (Native Americans): Totems represent ancestral and animal spirits, serve as protective symbols, and stand as significant monuments for communities.

Argentine Tango (Argentina): A sensual dance from Buenos Aires blending elegance with intensity, symbolizing themes of love, sorrow, and tension.

Peking Opera (China): A combination of singing, dancing, facial expressions, and acrobatics, telling stories from Chinese legends and history.

Didgeridoo (Australia): A traditional instrument of Australian Indigenous peoples, producing deep, resonant sounds and used in spiritual rituals.

Kuchipudi Dance (India): A classical Indian dance from Andhra Pradesh that merges theater, music, and dance to convey stories from Hindu epics.

Capoeira (Brazil): A mix of martial arts and dance, born from African slaves, characterized by rhythm and acrobatics, expressing strength and freedom.

Fado Music (Portugal): Melancholic Portuguese music focused on themes of "saudade" – longing and nostalgia, telling stories of love, separation, and dreams.

Gamelan Ensemble (Indonesia): A musical group with gongs, drums, and xylophones, used in religious ceremonies and celebrations in Bali and Java.

Carnival Samba (Brazil): A rhythmic dance from Rio de Janeiro, filled with energy and colors, central to the celebration of Carnival.

African Masks (Africa): Handcrafted masks used in rituals and spiritual ceremonies, representing ancestral spirits and mythological beings.

Flamenco Music (Spain): Intense guitar rhythms, singing, and rhythmic clapping (palmas) that accompany emotional Flamenco dances.

Polynesian Dances (Polynesia): Dances such as the haka from New Zealand express strength and connection to ancestors and nature; haka is also performed as a warrior dance.

Batik Art (Indonesia and Malaysia): A traditional textile art using wax and dye, creating unique patterns with deep cultural meanings.

Irish Dance: Energetic dances like "Riverdance" originating from Irish traditions, featuring characteristic footwork performed primarily with the feet.

Jazz (USA): A musical genre rooted in African American traditions, rich in improvisation and emotion, which has revolutionized music and culture worldwide.

•Subchapter 7.5: Famous Buildings and Their History

Great Pyramid of Giza (Egypt): Built around 2560 BCE as a tomb for Pharaoh Khufu, this is the only surviving wonder of the ancient world and continues to fascinate archaeologists.

Taj Mahal (India): A mausoleum built in the 17th century by Emperor Shah Jahan for his wife Mumtaz Mahal, symbolizing love and known for its stunning marble domes and gardens.

Eiffel Tower (France): Constructed for the 1889 World's Fair, it has become the symbol of Paris. Initially criticized, it is now celebrated as an icon of architecture.

Colosseum (Italy): This Roman amphitheater, completed in 80 CE, hosted games and gladiatorial contests and represents the grandeur of ancient Rome.

Machu Picchu (Peru): A hidden Incan city in the Andes rediscovered in 1911, it was likely a sacred site or summer residence for the Inca elite.

Statue of Liberty (USA): A gift from France to the U.S. in 1886, symbolizing freedom and hope, welcoming immigrants arriving in America.

Acropolis (Greece): The ancient citadel in Athens built in the 5th century BCE, home to the Parthenon, is a symbol of ancient Greece and the birthplace of democracy.

Great Wall of China (China): Spanning over 21,000 km, it was built to protect against invasions and stands as a symbol of ancient Chinese engineering and resilience.

Petra (Jordan): A rock-carved city by the Nabataeans, famous for the Al-Khazneh facade, it was a major trading hub on the caravan route.

Angkor Wat (Cambodia): The largest temple complex in the world, built in the 12th century and originally dedicated to Vishnu, it has become a symbol of Cambodia.

Notre-Dame Cathedral (France): This Gothic cathedral in Paris, built in the 13th century, is famous for its stained glass and architecture. Damaged by fire in 2019, it is undergoing restoration.

Potala Palace (Tibet): Built in the 17th century, it served as the Dalai Lamas' residence and is one of the highest palaces in the world, symbolizing Tibetan Buddhism.

Himeji Castle (Japan): Built in the 14th century and known as the "White Heron Castle" due to its appearance, it is one of Japan's oldest and best-preserved castles.

Buckingham Palace (United Kingdom): Expanded in the 18th century, it is the official residence of the British royal family and a renowned symbol of monarchy.

Blue Mosque (Turkey): Built in the 17th century in Istanbul, famous for its blue tiles and domes, it is a landmark of Islamic architecture.

Saint Basil's Cathedral (Russia): This colorful cathedral on Red Square in Moscow, built by Ivan the Terrible in the 16th century, is an icon of Russian architecture.

Burj Khalifa (United Arab Emirates): The tallest building in the world, completed in Dubai in 2010, it represents modern architectural achievement and development.

Sydney Opera House (Australia): This modernist opera house opened in 1973 with a roof resembling sails, symbolizing Australian architecture.

Stonehenge (United Kingdom): A prehistoric stone circle in England with an unknown purpose, likely used for ritual or astronomical functions.

Alhambra (Spain): A palace and fortress complex in Granada built by Muslim rulers, it is a masterpiece of Islamic architecture and art.

Chapter 8: Mysteries of Science

•Subchapter 8.1: Experiments That Changed the World

Millikan's Oil Drop Experiment – Measuring the Electron's Charge: Robert Millikan's oil drop experiment allowed for the first precise measurement of the electron's charge, paving the way for quantum physics.

Rutherford's Alpha Scattering Experiment – Discovery of the Atomic Nucleus: Ernest Rutherford's findings showed that atoms have a nucleus, reshaping the atomic model and leading to studies in nuclear energy.

Michelson-Morley Experiment – Disproving Ether: This experiment showed that ether, a hypothetical medium, does not exist, supporting Einstein's theories of relativity and transforming our understanding of space and time.

Pavlov's Conditioning Experiment – Classical Conditioning: Ivan Pavlov discovered the mechanics of conditioning, laying the groundwork for studying learning and behavior in humans and animals.

Curie Experiments on Radioactivity – Discovery of New Elements: Marie and Pierre Curie's work on radioactivity led to the discovery of polonium and radium, advancing nuclear medicine.

Herschel's Infrared Experiment – Extending the Spectrum: William Herschel discovered infrared light while experimenting with sunlight, expanding the electromagnetic spectrum and influencing astronomy.

Young's Double-Slit Experiment – Wave Nature of Light: Thomas Young's double-slit experiment proved light's wave properties, advancing quantum mechanics and optics.

Pasteur's Experiment – Disproving Spontaneous Generation: Louis Pasteur showed that microorganisms do not spontaneously arise, forming the basis for microbiology and pasteurization.

Mendel's Pea Plant Experiment – Inheritance Laws: Gregor Mendel's work with pea plants uncovered principles of genetic inheritance, founding modern genetics.

Avery's DNA Experiment – Genetic Blueprint Discovery: Avery's research demonstrated that DNA is the genetic material, marking a breakthrough in molecular biology.

Fleming's Discovery of Penicillin – Start of Antibiotics: Alexander Fleming's accidental discovery of penicillin launched the antibiotic era, revolutionizing medicine.

Watson and Crick's DNA Structure Discovery – The Double Helix: Supported by Rosalind Franklin's X-ray images, Watson and Crick revealed DNA's double-helix structure, transforming genetics.

Stanford Prison Experiment – Influence of Environment on Behavior: Philip Zimbardo's prison simulation showed the powerful effect of environment on human behavior, influencing social psychology.

Schrödinger's Cat Thought Experiment – Quantum Mechanics Paradox: Schrödinger's thought experiment illustrated the principle of superposition, highlighting the complexities of quantum mechanics.

Casimir Effect – Empty Space Interactions: Hendrik Casimir's experiment showed that empty space produces quantum fluctuations, advancing theories on quantum fields.

Milgram's Obedience Study – Power of Authority: Milgram's experiment revealed how individuals can follow harmful orders under authority, reshaping views on obedience.

Jane Elliott's "Blue Eyes/Brown Eyes" Exercise – Social Inequality: Elliott's experiment demonstrated the impact of discrimination, providing insights into prejudice and bias.

Fermi's Nuclear Reactor – Harnessing Atomic Energy: Enrico Fermi built the first nuclear reactor, sparking the development of nuclear power and influencing atomic research.

Haldane's "Primordial Soup" Experiment – Life Origins Theory: J.B.S. Haldane's studies on organic compounds explored theories of how life began, impacting origins-of-life research.

Milgram's "Small World" Experiment – Social Connections: Milgram's experiment on social networks led to the theory of "six degrees of separation," influencing network theory.

•Subchapter 8.2: The Most Controversial Scientific Theories

Darwin's Theory of Evolution: The idea that species evolve through natural selection sparked controversy in both religious and scientific circles, fueling an ongoing debate between creationism and evolution.

Quantum Mechanics and Heisenberg's Uncertainty Principle: The theory that it's impossible to simultaneously determine a particle's exact speed and position challenged classical views of reality and led to philosophical debates.

Big Bang Theory: The concept that the universe originated from a single point of infinite density initially faced significant criticism, particularly from religious groups and proponents of the steady-state theory.

Flat Earth Theory: Despite overwhelming evidence supporting Earth's round shape, some still advocate for a flat Earth model, sparking public debate and controversy.

Eugenics: This theory of controlling genetic selection to "improve" populations was widely criticized and exploited, especially during the Nazi era, leading to ethical and human rights abuses.

String Theory: The idea that all particles are actually vibrating strings in multiple dimensions remains controversial due to its lack of experimental confirmation.

Anthropic Principle: This theory suggests that the universe has properties suited to life, sparking debate over its implication that the universe might be "designed" for human existence.

Gaia Hypothesis: Proposing that Earth and its ecosystems act as a self-regulating organism, this idea is debated for attributing Earth anthropomorphic qualities.

Panspermia Theory: The hypothesis that life on Earth originated from outer space, potentially brought by meteors or comets, remains contentious as it challenges Earth-centric origin theories.

Multiverse Hypothesis: The theory that there are infinite parallel universes is controversial due to the lack of direct evidence for these other universes.

Transhumanism: The belief that technology can enhance human abilities and even transcend biological limitations raises ethical questions about identity and the essence of humanity.

Cold Fusion: The idea that nuclear reactions can occur at low temperatures faced widespread skepticism due to questionable experimental results, but it still inspires hope for new energy sources.

Water Memory Theory: The claim that water retains "memory" of substances it's contacted, forming the basis for homeopathy, remains disputed due to a lack of solid evidence.

Intelligent Design Theory: The notion that the complexity of the universe and life suggests a purposeful creator presents an alternative to evolution, generating controversy.

Geocentric Theory: This historical concept that Earth is the center of the universe was later disproven by heliocentrism but heavily influenced science and philosophy for centuries.

Simulation Hypothesis: The theory that reality might be a computer simulation raises philosophical and scientific debate, questioning the very nature of our reality.

Parapsychology (Telepathy, Telekinesis): Research into paranormal phenomena remains controversial due to a lack of conclusive evidence and scientific skepticism.

Intelligence as a Determinant of Success (IQ Theory): The idea that intelligence measured by IQ tests determines life success is debated due to test limitations and environmental influences.

Placebo Effect: The phenomenon where patients experience relief after receiving an inert substance challenges assumptions about the mind's role in healing.

Expanding Earth Theory: The hypothesis that Earth's volume is increasing is controversial, as it contradicts tectonic theories and lacks supporting evidence.

•Subchapter 8.3: Genetics and Unusual Mutations

Polydactyly: A mutation resulting in extra fingers or toes. It can run in families and does not typically impact health, though it is genetically uncommon.

Marfan Syndrome: A genetic disorder causing unusually long limbs, a slender build, and heart issues. People with Marfan syndrome often have tall stature.

Genetic Chimerism: A rare phenomenon in which a person has two distinct sets of DNA, often due to the fusion of two embryos at an early development stage.

Albinism: A genetic mutation leading to a lack of pigment in skin, hair, and eyes, making those affected more susceptible to vision problems and light sensitivity.

Waardenburg Syndrome: This condition causes blue eyes across racial groups, white patches of hair, and partial deafness due to effects on pigmentation and hearing.

Myostatin-Related Muscle Hypertrophy: A mutation in the MSTN gene results in excessive muscle growth without exercise, seen in some athletes and bodybuilders.

Hemophilia: A genetic blood clotting disorder causing difficulty in stopping bleeding, inherited recessively and affecting mostly men.

Ehlers-Danlos Syndrome (Rubber Man Syndrome): People with this mutation have extreme joint flexibility and can bend in ways others cannot due to connective tissue abnormalities.

Cyclopia: A rare mutation causing the development of one eye in the center of the face, typically lethal.

Osteogenesis Imperfecta (Brittle Bone Disease): This condition leads to fragile bones that break easily due to defective collagen.

Color Blindness: A mutation on the X chromosome causing difficulty in distinguishing colors, primarily affecting men's color perception.

Amelia (Limb Absence): The congenital absence of one or more limbs due to genetic mutations or environmental factors during pregnancy.

Hypertrichosis (Werewolf Syndrome): Excessive body hair due to a genetic mutation, giving affected individuals a "werewolf" appearance.

Angelman Syndrome: A mutation causing developmental delays, distinctive movements, and behavior resembling a "happy child" disposition.

Progeria: A mutation in the LMNA gene leads to premature aging, causing health issues typical of advanced age to appear in children.

Sirenomelia (Mermaid Syndrome): A mutation causing the legs to fuse, creating a "mermaid" appearance, often associated with severe health complications.

Ehlers-Danlos Syndrome: A connective tissue disorder resulting in elastic skin and joints, leading to easy bruising and bleeding issues.

Synesthesia: A condition where senses are mixed, such as seeing sounds or tasting colors, often due to unique neurological activity.

Lesch-Nyhan Syndrome: A mutation causing excessive uric acid buildup and self-injurious behaviors like biting lips and fingers.

Phenylketonuria (PKU): A mutation in the PAH gene prevents the metabolism of the amino acid phenylalanine, leading to neurological issues if not managed by diet.

•Subchapter 8.4: Breakthroughs in Medicine and Their Effects

Discovery of Penicillin by Alexander Fleming: In 1928, Fleming discovered penicillin, the first antibiotic, which launched the antibiotic era and enabled treatment of previously fatal bacterial infections.

Vaccination: The invention of the first smallpox vaccine by Edward Jenner in 1796 paved the way for other vaccines, eradicating or controlling many infectious diseases such as polio and measles.

Insulin as a Diabetes Treatment: The discovery and use of insulin in 1921 by Frederick Banting and Charles Best allowed for effective treatment of type 1 diabetes, extending the lives of many patients.

Discovery of DNA Structure by Watson and Crick: The discovery of the double-helix structure of DNA in 1953 opened up the field of molecular genetics, allowing for advances in gene therapy and genetic diagnostics.

Anesthesia: The introduction of general anesthesia in the 19th century revolutionized surgery, enabling complex operations without pain.

Kidney Dialysis: The development of dialysis machines by Willem Kolff in 1943 extended the lives of patients with kidney failure, allowing time until transplant became an option.

Organ Transplants: The first successful kidney transplant in 1954 sparked the development of transplant medicine, providing new treatments for organ failure.

Discovery of Helicobacter Pylori and Its Role in Ulcers: Barry Marshall and Robin Warren identified bacteria causing stomach ulcers, allowing for effective antibiotic treatment.

MRI (Magnetic Resonance Imaging): The development of MRI in the 1970s enabled safe internal body imaging, revolutionizing medical diagnostics.

Chemotherapy: The use of anti-cancer drugs since the 1940s has improved cancer treatment and significantly increased patient survival rates.

Gene Therapy: The introduction of gene therapy in the 1990s offered hope for treating genetic diseases by modifying genes to combat hereditary conditions.

HIV/AIDS Treatment with Antiretroviral Drugs: The development of antiretroviral therapy (ART) in the 1990s allowed for the management of HIV infections and significantly extended patients' lives.

Artificial Heart and Heart Support Devices: The invention of artificial hearts and pacemakers saved lives of patients with severe heart failure, enhancing their quality of life.

Cancer Immunotherapy: The development of therapies that stimulate the immune system to fight cancer, such as monoclonal antibody treatments, has increased the effectiveness of cancer treatment.

Artificial Trachea (Burn Treatment): A breakthrough surgery involving a stem cell-coated artificial trachea enabled treatment of severe airway injuries.

Endoscopy and Laparoscopy: The introduction of internal imaging techniques without large incisions allowed for minimally invasive surgeries and reduced recovery times.

Advances in Anti-Seizure Medications: The development of drugs like carbamazepine and valproic acid has significantly improved quality of life for people with epilepsy.

Biologic Drugs: Biologic therapies, such as TNF inhibitors for rheumatoid arthritis, reduced inflammation and improved mobility in patients.

Use of CRISPR for Gene Editing: CRISPR enables precise gene editing, opening new avenues in treating genetic diseases and advancing medical research.

Surgical Robotics (e.g., Da Vinci System): Robotic surgery allows for complex procedures with precision beyond traditional surgery, reducing risks of complications.

Subchapter 8.5: Incredible Laws of Physics

Newton's Law of Gravity: Newton formulated the law of universal gravitation, explaining why objects attract each other. This law revolutionized our understanding of celestial and terrestrial movements.

Heisenberg's Uncertainty Principle: In quantum mechanics, this principle states that it's impossible to precisely measure both the position and momentum of a particle simultaneously, challenging intuitive understandings of reality.

Einstein's Theory of General Relativity (Universal Gravitation): Einstein demonstrated that gravity is the curvature of spacetime, explaining phenomena like the bending of light by massive objects and transforming physics.

Maxwell's Laws of Electromagnetism: Maxwell's equations unify electricity and magnetism, forming the foundation of electromagnetic waves, such as light, and paving the way for communication technology.

Law of Conservation of Energy: Energy cannot be created or destroyed, only converted from one form to another, a foundational principle across physical and chemical processes.

Law of Entropy (Second Law of Thermodynamics): Entropy, or disorder, always increases in a closed system, explaining why processes tend toward chaos and systems naturally degrade over time.

Wave-Particle Duality Principle: Light and other subatomic particles exhibit properties of both waves and particles, a principle central to quantum mechanics that reshapes our understanding of matter.

Law of Superposition: In quantum mechanics, particles can exist in multiple states simultaneously until observed. This principle underlies quantum technology and computing.

Laws of Reflection and Refraction of Light: These laws explain how light behaves when passing through different materials, forming the basis of optics and technologies like lenses and microscopes.

Archimedes' Principle: The principle of buoyancy states that an object submerged in a fluid experiences an upward force equal to the weight of the displaced fluid, explaining why objects float or sink.

Huygens' Principle: Waves propagate in space as a series of secondary spherical waves, explaining phenomena like diffraction and wave interference.

Coulomb's Law: This law states that the electrostatic force between two charged objects is proportional to the product of their charges and inversely proportional to the square of the distance between them, fundamental in electrodynamics.

Bernoulli's Principle: In hydrodynamics, this principle states that a fluid's speed is inversely proportional to its pressure, explaining how planes achieve lift and influencing fluid dynamics.

Hubble's Law: The principle that the universe is expanding, with galaxies moving apart at speeds proportional to their distance, foundational in cosmology and evidence of the Big Bang.

Fermat's Principle (Least Time): Light follows the path that takes the least time, a fundamental law in optics applied in lens and mirror design.

Wien's Displacement Law: This law describes how the peak wavelength of a body's emitted radiation varies with temperature, foundational in thermal physics.

Kepler's Laws of Planetary Motion: Johannes Kepler's three laws describe the motion of planets around the Sun, advancing astronomy and celestial mechanics.

Einstein's Photoelectric Law: This law explains the ejection of electrons from a metal surface when exposed to light, forming the basis for quantum mechanics and technologies like photoelectric cells.

Joule's Law of Heating: Explains that conductors heat up due to current flow, a fundamental principle in electrical engineering and heating technology.

Zeroth Law of Thermodynamics: States that if two bodies are in thermal equilibrium with a third body, they are in thermal equilibrium with each other, key to understanding temperature and thermal equilibrium.

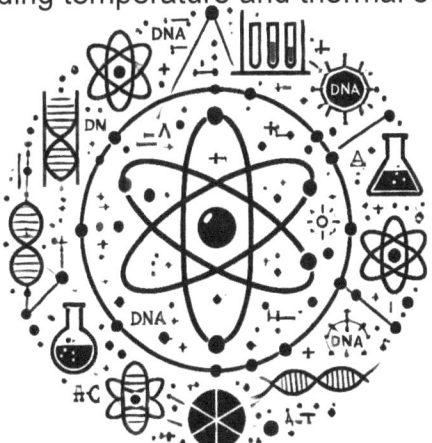

Chapter 9: Technologies of the Future

•Subchapter 9.1: Artificial Intelligence and Robotics

Autonomous Vehicles: Advances in artificial intelligence are paving the way for autonomous cars, drones, and delivery vehicles, promising to transform transportation, reduce accidents, and improve overall mobility.

Medical Robotics: Robotics in healthcare, including surgical assistance systems like Da Vinci, rehabilitation robots, and exoskeletons for patient support, are enhancing treatment precision and broadening healthcare capabilities.

AI in Medical Diagnostics: Algorithms analyzing medical images and patient data accelerate disease detection, aiding in accurate diagnoses for conditions such as cancer and expanding healthcare access.

Industry 4.0 and Factory Automation: AI-equipped robots increase production efficiency, reduce costs, and minimize human error, making manufacturing processes faster and more reliable.

Social and Companion Robots: Robots such as Pepper and Sophia, designed to recognize emotions and engage in conversation, hold potential for elder care and are increasingly used in educational and therapeutic support.

Image and Facial Recognition: Image recognition algorithms contribute to security and diagnostics but raise privacy concerns and ethical considerations.

Internet of Things (IoT) with AI Integration: AI-driven IoT enables "smart" management of buildings, homes, and appliances, enhancing energy efficiency and simplifying daily life.

Creative Artificial Intelligence: AI creating music, art, literature, and even architectural designs introduces new possibilities in creative fields, while also raising questions about the nature of creativity itself.

Advanced Brain-Computer Interfaces: Technologies enabling direct brain-to-computer communication may support people with paralysis and open new avenues for human augmentation.

AI in Education: Adaptive AI educational tools that tailor learning to individual student needs are paving the way for personalized, accessible education for all.

AI in Finance and Economics: AI systems predicting market trends, analyzing investments, and managing finances could lead to greater economic stability but also increase automation in the financial industry.

Rescue and Assistance Robots: Autonomous robots designed for challenging environments, such as disaster zones, are capable of searching through debris and assisting in rescue operations.

Advanced General Intelligence (AGI): The concept of AGI, an AI with cognitive capabilities comparable to humans, presents ethical challenges regarding control and the potential societal impact of such powerful tools.

AI in Agriculture: AI can aid in crop monitoring, yield prediction, and optimizing irrigation, promoting more efficient and sustainable farming practices.

Environmental Cleanup Robots: Underwater and terrestrial robots that collect waste and monitor environmental health help protect ecosystems by, for example, reducing plastic pollution in oceans.

Cybersecurity with AI: AI detects cyber threats, analyzes anomalies, and defends against cyber-attacks, which is essential in today's digitalized world.

Personal AI Assistants: Systems like Alexa, Siri, and Google Assistant help manage daily schedules, provide reminders, and answer questions, making them integral to smart home systems.

AI in Natural Language Processing (NLP): AI's ability to process human language revolutionizes communication, enabling translation, text analysis, and interaction with devices.

Medical Microrobots: Tiny robots capable of operating inside the human body to deliver drugs to targeted locations or perform microscopic procedures are opening new frontiers in precision medicine.

Autonomous Military Systems and Drones: The advancement of drones and autonomous warfare systems could revolutionize military operations, yet it brings ethical challenges around AI's use in combat.

•Subchapter 9.2: The Future of Space Travel

Colonizing Mars: Ambitious plans led by NASA, SpaceX, and other space agencies aim to establish the first permanent bases on Mars, enabling long-term habitation and research on the Red Planet.

Nuclear-Powered Spacecraft: Nuclear propulsion could revolutionize interplanetary travel, significantly reducing travel time to Mars and making missions to farther planets in the Solar System feasible.

Space Hotels and Space Tourism: Companies like Blue Origin and Virgin Galactic are developing commercial space flights, and future space hotels could offer a new kind of tourism for thrill-seekers.

Lunar Exploration and Moon Bases: NASA's Artemis program plans to return humans to the Moon and establish a permanent lunar base, serving as a stepping stone for Mars exploration and other deep-space missions.

Photon Propulsion (Light-Based Drive): Photon-based propulsion technology could enable faster interstellar travel, using the power of light to propel spacecraft through space.

Self-Sustaining Bases on Mars and the Moon: Future bases on Mars and the Moon will aim to be self-sufficient, producing oxygen, water, and energy, which will support long-term stays for astronauts and explorers.

Terraforming Planets: The concept of altering the atmosphere and conditions on other planets, such as Mars, to make them habitable is a long-term goal in space exploration.

Travel to Exoplanets: The discovery of thousands of exoplanets in "habitable zones" has made the development of interstellar travel technology crucial for exploring new worlds.

Artificial Gravity on Spacecraft: Creating artificial gravity on spacecraft could enable long-duration missions, improving astronaut comfort and health during extended space travel.

Space Stations and Platforms: Plans for next-generation space stations orbiting the Moon and Mars will support research and the expansion of human presence beyond Earth.

Building Space Telescopes for Exploring the Universe: Space-based telescopes will allow for more precise observations of exoplanets, black holes, and distant galaxies, enhancing our understanding of the cosmos.

Asteroid Resource Extraction: Mining precious metals, ice, and other resources from asteroids could support self-sufficient space missions and help develop a future space-based economy.

Unmanned Missions to Distant Solar System Regions: Planned missions to Jupiter, Saturn, and their moons, such as Europa and Enceladus, may reveal conditions suitable for life.

Exploring Subsurface Oceans: Landers and probes on icy moons like Europa and Enceladus aim to search for signs of life in hidden oceans beneath their icy surfaces.

Multi-Generational Spacecraft: Ships capable of carrying generations of humans over centuries would enable travel to the farthest reaches of the universe, where journeys exceed human lifespans.

Antimatter Technology: Propulsion using antimatter could accelerate spacecraft to extreme speeds, making interstellar travel feasible within relatively short timeframes.

Wormholes and Time Travel: While still theoretical, research on spacetime warping and wormholes may one day unlock the potential for time travel.

Fast-Access Probes (e.g., Starshot): Projects like Breakthrough Starshot, which envisions laser-propelled mini-probes, could enable rapid missions to nearby stars such as Proxima Centauri.

Space Debris Management: The growing amount of space debris poses risks to future missions, prompting the development of technology to clean Earth's orbit and recycle space waste.

Space Colonies on Orbital Stations: In the future, permanent human colonies with self-sustaining ecosystems could exist on large orbital space stations, opening new possibilities for civilization beyond Earth.

•Subchapter 9.3: Nanotechnology and Its Applications

Nanomedicine: Nanoparticles delivering drugs directly to diseased cells enable targeted cancer treatments, minimizing side effects on healthy cells.

Nanorobots in the Bloodstream: Nanorobots can be programmed to repair damage in the body, such as blood clots, infections, or tissue damage, by working at the cellular level.

Molecular Diagnostics: Nano-sensors can detect disease biomarkers at early stages, allowing for early diagnosis and precise treatment of diseases like cancer and infections.

Water Filtration: Nanofilters can remove the smallest contaminants, bacteria, and viruses from water, increasing access to clean water—especially crucial for communities without reliable resources.

Data Storage and Transmission: Nanotechnology can increase digital storage capacity and data transmission speeds, potentially revolutionizing electronics and the IT sector.

Nanotechnology in Cosmetics: Nanoparticles in products like sunscreens and skincare enhance absorption and improve protection against UV radiation.

Nanotechnology in Food Industry: Nanoencapsulation helps preserve nutrients and extend shelf life, enabling the creation of food with enhanced health properties.

Nanocoatings in Electronics: Nanocoatings increase the durability and scratch-resistance of device screens like smartphones and tablets.

Nano-Energy Technology: Advances in nanotechnology support more efficient batteries and supercapacitors, improving energy storage capacity and enabling more compact devices.

Antibacterial Nanocoatings: Nanotechnology enables the creation of surfaces with antibacterial properties used in hospitals, helping to prevent the spread of infections.

Nanocomposites in Construction: Nanoparticles produce stronger, lighter building materials, enhancing structural safety and reducing construction costs.

Nanotechnology Catalysts: Nanoparticle catalysts accelerate chemical reactions, increasing industrial process efficiency and reducing raw material use.

Nanomaterials for Burn Treatment: Advanced bandages containing nanoparticles help skin regenerate faster and reduce infection risk, essential for burn treatment.

Nanotechnology in Agriculture: Nano-formulated fertilizers and pesticides increase efficiency and reduce environmental impact by minimizing the necessary doses.

Nanotechnology in Textiles: Nanoparticles give fabrics water-resistant, antibacterial, and stain-resistant properties, improving garment durability and functionality.

Conductors and Nanostructured Materials: Nanoparticles used in conductors improve electrical conductivity, making them useful in modern electronic circuits.

Nanoparticles in Biomedical Research: Nanoparticles serve as molecular imaging markers, enabling precise localization of disease processes and better treatment planning.

Air Pollution Remediation: Nanofilters remove toxic substances from the air, enhancing air quality and reducing public health impacts from pollution.

Nanotechnology in Defense and Weaponry: Protective nanopowders and nanosensors are used in military technology, enhancing equipment durability and threat detection.

3D Printing with Nanoparticles: 3D printing with nanomaterials allows for strong, precise structures, with applications in medicine, construction, and industrial production.

•Subchapter 9.4: Renewable Energy and Eco-Innovations

Solar Energy and Photovoltaic Panels: Modern photovoltaic panels with enhanced efficiency and flexibility are capable of powering residential, industrial, and transport applications, significantly reducing CO_2 emissions.

Wind Energy: Advances in wind turbine technology make onshore and offshore wind farms increasingly popular as sustainable alternatives to fossil fuels.

Geothermal Power Plants: Harnessing Earth's internal heat as an energy source is a promising technology, especially in geothermal-rich countries like Iceland and the Philippines.

Wave and Tidal Energy: Power plants that utilize the motion of waves and tides can deliver consistent energy in coastal areas, supporting sustainable electricity production.

Energy Storage: Next-generation batteries, such as lithium-iron and sodium-based storage, allow for long-term energy storage, which is crucial for supporting renewable energy sources.

Electromobility and Electric Vehicles: Developing electric cars, buses, and other vehicles reduces air pollution and reliance on fossil fuels.

Zero-Emission Homes: Buildings designed to minimize energy usage, equipped with solar panels and heat recovery systems, are becoming the standard for sustainable architecture.

Second-Generation Biofuels: Produced from agricultural and forestry waste, these biofuels reduce emissions compared to conventional fuels while supporting a circular economy.

Smart Grid Systems: Smart energy grids optimize usage and adjust energy production to demand, enhancing energy supply efficiency.

Passive Heating and Cooling Systems: Systems like solar collectors and heat pumps regulate building temperatures naturally, reducing overall energy needs.

Water and Gray Water Recycling: Gray water recycling systems enable households to reuse water, decreasing water consumption and waste.

Modern Building Materials: Eco-friendly materials like green concrete, clay, and bamboo are more durable, renewable, and have a lower carbon footprint, supporting sustainable construction.

Hydrogen Fuel Cells: Hydrogen combustion, which emits only water vapor, offers the potential for a carbon-free fuel source.

Hydroponic and Vertical Farming: These agricultural techniques save space, water, and energy, promoting sustainable food production, especially in urban areas.

Eco-Friendly Plastics and Biodegradable Packaging: Biodegradable packaging materials made from algae, mushrooms, or corn replace plastics and break down more easily in the environment.

Green Roofs and Walls: Vegetation on rooftops and building walls insulates, absorbs CO_2, reduces urban pollution, and supports biodiversity.

Regenerative Agriculture: Farming practices that restore soil health, increase carbon storage, and enhance biodiversity help combat climate change.

Selective Waste Collection and Recycling Systems: Advanced sorting and recycling technologies, including optical and robotic systems, increase the efficiency of material processing.

Environmental Bioremediation: Using microorganisms to eliminate toxins and pollutants from soil and water naturally and safely cleanses the environment.

Biomass Energy: Using biomass, including wood, plant waste, and algae, as a renewable energy source helps reduce carbon emissions and fossil fuel dependence.

- **Subchapter 9.5: Military Technologies and Their Development**

Drones and Unmanned Aerial Vehicles (UAVs): Combat, reconnaissance, and logistical drones are transforming military operations by enabling safe and precise remote actions.

Autonomous Combat Systems: Advances in artificial intelligence allow for autonomous robots capable of independently detecting and neutralizing threats.

Laser Weapons: Laser-based weaponry can target drones, missiles, and aircraft, offering a direct means of defense without expending traditional ammunition.

Exoskeletons for Soldiers: Advanced exoskeletons enhance soldiers' strength, endurance, and mobility, enabling longer operations in challenging environments.

Hypersonic Weapons: Hypersonic missiles, traveling over five times the speed of sound, are challenging to intercept and could revolutionize defense strategy.

Cybersecurity Systems: The development of advanced cybersecurity measures is crucial as cyber threats become one of the biggest challenges facing modern armed forces.

Stealth Technologies: Applied in aircraft, ships, and drones, stealth techniques reduce radar, thermal, and acoustic signatures, making them harder to detect.

Microwave Weapons: Microwave systems can neutralize drones and other devices by disrupting electronics, proving effective in defending against drone swarms.

AI in Intelligence Analysis: Artificial intelligence aids in analyzing large quantities of intelligence data, expediting decision-making and real-time threat identification.

Military Satellites and Space Surveillance: Satellites monitoring enemy movements and providing accurate positioning are integral to modern military operations.

Nanotechnology in Personal Protection: Nanomaterials used in helmets and bulletproof vests are lightweight yet strong, enhancing soldier safety without adding weight.

Unmanned Naval Vessels: Unmanned marine vessels for reconnaissance, mine removal, and combat tasks offer flexible, safer operations on the water.

Biotechnology for Soldier Endurance: Advanced pharmacological solutions and biotechnology can enhance soldiers' endurance and perception, valuable for extended missions.

Missile Defense Systems: Systems like THAAD and Patriot effectively intercept ballistic missiles, protecting against potential missile attacks.

Adaptive Camouflage Technologies: Materials that change color and structure based on surroundings can make soldiers and equipment nearly invisible on the battlefield.

Amphibious and Autonomous Land/Water Vehicles: Autonomous vehicles that operate on various terrains support military logistics and rapid supply transport.

Electromagnetic Weapons: Electromagnetic pulse (EMP) generation can disable electronics within a targeted area, potentially paralyzing enemy command and control systems.

Microrobots for Rescue Operations: Small robots capable of navigating tight spaces assist in search and rescue missions and explosive ordinance disposal.

3D Printing on the Battlefield: Field-based 3D printing of spare parts and tools allows for quick equipment repairs, enhancing mobility and operational independence.

Acoustic Weapons: Acoustic technologies, such as sonic cannons, are used for crowd control, disorienting opponents, or protecting strategic assets.

Chapter 10: Daily Life and Surprising Facts

• **Subchapter 10.1: The Strangest Guinness World Records**

Most Spoons Balanced on the Face: Aaron Cauna set the record in 2016 by balancing 17 spoons on his face, impressing onlookers with his balancing skill.

Largest Grilled Cheese Sandwich: A team of chefs in the United States created a massive 146-kilogram grilled cheese sandwich, becoming a culinary sensation and record-breaker.

Longest Fingernails: Ayanna Williams grew her nails for 28 years, reaching a total length of 731 cm before finally trimming them and securing her record.

Most Tattoos of a Single Name in 24 Hours: A man set the record by tattooing the name "Katie" on himself 200 times as a declaration of love.

Largest Chewing Gum Collection: Barry Chappell amassed over 95,000 pieces of chewing gum, forming a massive ball over 1.5 meters in diameter, setting an unusual record.

Longest Time Holding a Scorpion in the Mouth: Circus performer Keerat Singh held a scorpion in his mouth for 37 seconds, demonstrating courage and patience.

World's Longest Tongue: Nick Stoeberl from California holds the record with a 10.1 cm tongue, which allows him to lick his nose and impress friends.

Most Pencils Held in the Mouth: Durga Raghavendra from India managed to fit 459 pencils in his mouth at once, amazing onlookers.

Largest Collection of Dog Outfits: Record-holder Pampered Pet gathered over 1,000 outfits for her dog, setting the record for the largest collection of pet clothes.

Largest Water Snake Dance: At a water park in China, 1,000 people formed a human "water snake," setting a new Guinness World Record.

Most Oreo Cookies Stacked in the Mouth: Simon Neille holds the record for fitting 28 Oreo cookies in his mouth simultaneously.

Largest Santa Claus Costume: A team in Moscow created a Santa suit standing 22 meters tall, which became a holiday attraction and record-holder.

Largest Garlic Head Collection: A record-holder gathered 4,200 garlic heads from around the world, creating an impressive and unique collection.

Longest Hugging Marathon: A couple in Thailand set the record by embracing for 58 hours, breaking previous hugging records.

Most T-Shirts Worn at Once: Ted Hastings donned 260 T-shirts simultaneously, a feat that took hours and required assistance.

Longest Single Nail on One Finger: Shridhar Chillal from India grew a single nail for over 60 years, reaching a length of more than 2 meters and earning a unique record.

Largest Bubble Gum Collection: Michelle Laprise gathered over 150,000 different types of bubble gum from around the world, setting a remarkable collecting record.

Longest Hula Hoop Marathon: Cami Boehme from Utah hula-hooped continuously for 74 hours, showing incredible endurance and setting a new record.

Longest Breath-Holding Time: Budimir Šobat set the record by holding his breath for 24 minutes and 37 seconds, astounding the world.

Largest Pencil Sculpture: A record-holder created a sculpture over 12 meters long using pencils, achieving both an artistic and record-breaking feat.

•Subchapter 10.2: Origins of Popular Phrases and Sayings

"Casting pearls before swine": This phrase originates from the Bible (Gospel of Matthew) and is a metaphor for wasting something valuable or offering advice to those who won't appreciate it.

"Marked by the tooth of time": This saying describes the aging or decay of objects over time, personifying time as something that "gnaws away" at things.

"Caught red-handed": This expression dates back to medieval law, where catching someone in the act of committing a crime was essential for conviction.

"Holy peace": This saying reflects the idea that peace is elusive and almost sacred in a chaotic life, making it highly valued.

"Crocodile tears": Based on the old belief that crocodiles weep while eating their prey, this phrase symbolizes fake emotions or insincere regret.

"Stirring up a hornet's nest": This means creating disturbance or trouble. It stems from the idea that disturbing a hornet's nest creates chaos, much like poking an ant hill with a stick.

"Pulling something up by the roots": Refers to the complete and permanent removal of something, just like pulling a plant out with its entire root system.

"All roads lead to Rome": This originates from the Roman Empire, when most roads literally led to Rome, symbolizing the idea that there are many ways to reach the same goal.

"Keeping one's fingers crossed": This custom dates back to ancient times when it was believed that crossing fingers brought good luck and warded off evil spirits.

"Trojan horse": This phrase comes from Homer's Iliad, where the Greeks used a wooden horse filled with soldiers to infiltrate Troy, symbolizing betrayal or hidden threats.

"Not buying a pig in a poke": This expression comes from times when merchants deceived buyers by selling them a cat in a bag instead of the promised item.

"Black and white": This saying originates from the traditional black ink on white paper, symbolizing clarity and unequivocal understanding.

"Empty promises": This phrase refers to beautiful but untrue promises, likened to something charming (cacanki in Polish) but lacking substance.

"Bull in a china shop": This expression represents someone who is clumsy or lacks subtlety, causing damage as a bull would in a store full of porcelain.

"Having something on one's conscience": This phrase stems from religious beliefs that conscience stores moral responsibilities that weigh down one's soul.

"Casting a glance": Means to take a quick look at something. Historically, this could have represented a brief yet attentive observation.

"Having an axe to grind": This expression originated when wood stumps were used as markers for resolving neighborhood disputes or establishing boundaries.

"The last straw": This phrase originates from a metaphor about excess, where the last straw causes a spill, symbolizing a breaking point.

"Throwing down the gauntlet": This phrase originates from the chivalric tradition of throwing down a glove as a challenge to a duel, symbolizing an invitation to confrontation.

"Having two left hands": This phrase describes someone who is clumsy, especially in manual tasks, suggesting that having "two left hands" makes effective action difficult.

•Subchapter 10.3: Everyday Items and Their Unknown Histories

Matches: Originally invented in 6th century China as sulfur-coated sticks, matches evolved into safer versions with the invention of phosphorus matches in the 19th century.

Toilet Paper: In ancient times, people used leaves, stones, or fabrics for hygiene. Toilet paper specially made for this purpose appeared in China in the 14th century, with commercial production starting in the 19th century.

Ballpoint Pen: In 1938, Hungarian journalist László Bíró invented the first practical ballpoint pen, revolutionizing the way people wrote.

Takeaway Coffee Cup: The paper cup with a plastic lid was designed in the 1960s by Dixie Cup, making it safe to carry drinks, especially for drivers.

Microwave Oven: Percy Spencer accidentally discovered microwave heating when a chocolate bar melted in his pocket while he worked near radar equipment in 1945.

Umbrella: The first umbrellas were used in ancient China, Egypt, and Greece as sun protection, with rain umbrellas emerging in the 18th century.

Post-it Notes: Invented accidentally by chemist Spencer Silver, who developed a low-tack adhesive in the 1970s, the sticky notes became a practical and popular office tool.

Paper Clip: Although Johan Vaaler is often credited with inventing it, earlier versions of the paper clip existed, and the modern design became widely used over time.

Sunglasses: The first sunglasses were used by Chinese judges in the 12th century to hide their eyes, while their sun-protection role began in the 20th century.

Flush Toilet: The first flush toilet was invented by John Harington in the 16th century for Queen Elizabeth I, but it only became widespread in the 19th century.

Rubik's Cube: Invented in 1974 by Hungarian architect Ernő Rubik as a teaching tool for geometry, it later became a globally popular puzzle.

Chocolate Bars: Originally consumed as a bitter drink by the Maya and Aztecs, chocolate in bar form emerged in the 19th century with added sugar and cocoa butter.

Credit Cards: Inspired by loyalty card systems, Diners Club introduced the first credit card in 1950, revolutionizing shopping and payments.

Toothbrush: Ancient Egyptians and Chinese used twigs as cleaning tools. The first toothbrush with natural bristles appeared in China in the 15th century.

Wristwatch: Invented for Queen Elizabeth I of Hungary by horologist Robert Dudley in the 16th century, wristwatches became common in the 20th century.

Mason Jar: John Landis Mason invented airtight jars in the 19th century, allowing for longer food preservation and sparking a home canning trend.

Aspirin: Ancient Egyptians used willow bark infusions as early forms of aspirin. Modern aspirin was developed by Felix Hoffmann for Bayer in 1897.

Mobile Phone: The first portable mobile phone, created by Motorola in 1973, was large and costly, with today's smartphones being the result of decades of technological advancement.

Eraser: Initially, bread crumbs were used to erase pencil marks. In 1770, Edward Nairne accidentally discovered that pieces of rubber worked better.

Thermal Mug: Invented in the 1980s by Jim Berns, thermal mugs were designed to keep beverages hot or cold, quickly gaining popularity among active individuals.

Subchapter 10.4: Unusual Laws and Regulations Around the World

Switzerland's Ban on Flushing Toilets After 10 p.m. in Apartment Buildings: In some Swiss cantons, flushing the toilet at night is considered noise pollution, which can result in a fine.

Singapore's Ban on Chewing Gum: The import and sale of chewing gum are banned to prevent littering in the city, which prioritizes cleanliness.

No Penalty for Escaping Prison in Denmark: Danish law does not impose additional punishment for attempted prison escapes, recognizing freedom as a natural human desire.

Canada's Ban on Writing Checks Under 25 Cents: In certain Canadian provinces, writing checks for amounts under 25 cents is prohibited to reduce unnecessary transactions.

Japan's Waistline Regulations: Japanese law mandates regular waist measurements for individuals over 40, with overweight individuals receiving health guidance to address potential issues.

High Heel Ban in Ancient Sites of Greece: High heels are banned at ancient sites, such as the Acropolis, to protect these historic monuments.

Australia's Ban on Kangaroos at Parliament: Following incidents where kangaroos entered parliamentary grounds, a rule was enacted to restrict their access.

Saudi Arabia's Ban on Public Photography Without Permission: To protect privacy, taking photos in public spaces without the consent of all individuals in the photo is prohibited.

UK's Ban on Armor in Parliament: A historic law states that individuals in full armor are barred from entering Parliament, originally intended to prevent medieval disputes from escalating.

San Francisco's Ban on Washing Cars With a Hose: To conserve water, it is prohibited to wash cars with a garden hose, allowing only pressure washers or buckets.

Venezuela's Ban on Political Names for Children: In response to a trend of naming children after political figures, authorities placed restrictions on such practices.

Canada's Prohibition on Flushing Toilets Before 7 a.m. and After 10 p.m. in Quebec: To avoid noise disruption, flushing toilets during specific hours is restricted in Quebec.

Oklahoma's Ban on Making Faces at Dogs: This law aims to protect animals from potential stress by prohibiting residents from making faces or "scaring" dogs.

South Korea's Ban on Writing Names in Red Ink: Due to cultural beliefs, writing someone's name in red ink is associated with wishing death upon them, making it a serious taboo.

Bolivia's Restriction on Married Women Drinking More Than One Glass of Wine: This law, intended to prevent "improper" behavior, has sparked protests over gender discrimination.

Germany's Requirement to Carry Fuel on Highways: Running out of fuel on the autobahn is a punishable offense, as it can disrupt traffic and pose a safety risk.

Spain's Ban on Wearing Swimsuits Off the Beach: In Barcelona, wearing swimwear outside the beach is illegal, with fines issued to maintain urban decorum.

India's Selfie Ban in Certain Public Places: To enhance safety, some areas in India have restricted selfies to prevent accidents in risky locations.

Switzerland's Ban on Washing Cars on Sundays: Out of respect for Sunday as a day of rest, washing cars is prohibited to avoid disturbing the neighbors.

Finland's Income-Based Speeding Fines: Traffic fines are adjusted according to the driver's income, making penalties fairer and appropriately impactful for higher earners.

•Subsection 10.5: Fascinating Facts About Human Customs

Eating With Hands in India: Eating with hands in India is seen as a natural way to connect with food, emphasizing a personal bond with what is consumed—a practice deeply rooted in regional traditions.

Cheek Sniffing in Greenland (Kunikk): In Inuit culture, sniffing a loved one's cheeks is an expression of affection and closeness, symbolizing an emotional bond.

Tarantella Dance in Italy: This traditional southern Italian folk dance was believed to protect against tarantula bites, becoming an iconic symbol of Italian culture and vibrancy.

Honoring Ancestors' Spirits in Japan: During the Obon festival, Japanese people pay homage to their ancestors, believing their spirits visit the home, with rituals helping them find peace.

Drumming in Colombia: In San Basilio de Palenque, residents believe intense drumming calls on ancestral spirits, with drumming rituals serving as a form of connection with the afterlife.

Leather Dance in Romania: In Romanian tradition, men dance with calfskin belts, symbolically warding off evil spirits and ensuring protection for the coming year.

Fire Ceremony in Peru (Inti Raymi): Held annually in Cusco in honor of the sun god, this Inca festival celebrates the beginning of winter and includes prayers for a good harvest.

Flower Offerings in Thai Buddhist Temples: Thais present flowers and incense in temples, believing this will bring blessings and a prosperous life under the protection of benevolent spirits.

Building Circular Homes in China (Tulou): In Fujian, multi-story round communal homes, called tulou, represent family unity and community while offering protection against evil spirits.

Drinking Mate in Argentina: Mate drinkers follow traditional sharing rituals, which promote social bonding and create a strong sense of community.

Dancing with Spider Props in Spain (Fiesta de los Cangrejos): In Andalusia, celebrations feature dancing with spider-like props, symbolizing the release of negative energy.

Jumping Over Babies in Spain (El Colacho): In Burgos, men dressed as devils jump over newborns to ward off evil spirits and ensure their health and safety.

Throwing Vines in Bolivia (Boleadoras): In some Bolivian regions, families playfully toss vines at one another to symbolize friendship and trust.

Giving Coins in Greece: Newlyweds receive coins thrown at their feet, symbolizing wishes for prosperity and wealth in their marriage.

The Scarf Dance in Ireland: During Irish celebrations, couples exchange scarves in a dance to represent love and commitment, a traditional blessing for the union.

Cultivating White Threads in Thailand: At the "Sukwan" ceremony, white threads are tied around participants' wrists to symbolize protection and blessings from guardian spirits.

Dance of Joy in Nigeria (Gidan Sharo): Young men dance to drum rhythms to display their strength and maturity, a ritual marking their transition into adulthood.

Walking Through Flour in Mauritius: Newlyweds in Mauritius walk through flour as a symbol of purity and new beginnings, an essential part of wedding ceremonies.

Wearing Snow Masks in Mongolia: During winter rituals, masks representing animals and spirits are worn to bring luck and protection against evil forces.

Walking with a Hen in New Zealand: In parts of New Zealand, a hen symbolizes care and protection, and locals attach hen figurines to fences as a lucky talisman.

What the Facts Are You Talking About? is a book that unveils fascinating aspects of the world that we often overlook. From scientific mysteries and the stories behind everyday objects to incredible laws in far-off corners of the globe, this book takes readers on an extraordinary journey that both inspires and astonishes.

Each chapter is filled with carefully selected facts that reveal just how rich and diverse our world is. Guinness World Records, cultural rituals, and unusual human habits offer a fresh perspective on life, while quirky facts about the origins of popular expressions add flair to everyday conversation.

This book is a perfect read for anyone who loves learning new things—those fascinated by the variety of the world around us and eager to understand how people worldwide create traditions, customs, and remarkable stories. What the Facts Are You Talking About? is a collection of stories about an astonishing world full of unsolved mysteries, surprising scientific discoveries, and customs that, while sometimes strange, paint a vibrant picture of reality.

Ideal for curious minds, this book invites readers to see the world from a new perspective and explore how various aspects of culture, history, and science shape our lives. It's also a reminder that, although daily life might seem ordinary, it holds many surprises within.

Thank you for choosing this book! We hope it has brought value, insights, and perhaps a little inspiration to your life. At Life Style Daily, we're always looking to improve, and your thoughts truly matter. If you enjoyed the book—or if you have ideas on how we can make it even better—we'd be grateful if you could take a moment to leave a review or share your feedback.

Your support helps us continue to bring you new and meaningful content. Thank you for being part of our journey!

Warm regards,

Life Style Daily

www.ingramcontent.com/pod-product-compliance
Lightning Source LLC
LaVergne TN
LVHW021054100526
838202LV00083B/5851